The Wonders of Life

The Wonders of Life

Ida Lyon

DD BOOKS
Publishers for New Generations

The Wonders of Life

by ***Ida Lyon***

Price: ₹ 250/-

ISBN: 9789359579962

DD Books, Delhi

www.ddbookshub.com

ddsalesglobal@gmail.com

Printed in Republic of India

Table of Content

The Joy of Living

Life should be nothing less than a source of joy for us—not a superficial, fleeting imitation, but a genuine, effervescent joy that penetrates to the core of our being and transports us beyond the narrow confines of our outward existence into the vastness and splendor of universal life, with which our own is intimately and inseparably connected.

There is likely no one, however dire their circumstances, who hasn't, at some point, experienced the power of this feeling of joy in simply being alive. Yet, instead of cherishing it and summoning it forth repeatedly, it often flits by as a transient glimpse of a gift meant for us to hold dear in our hearts—a power to elevate us above adversity into more favorable circumstances.

This joy is often overshadowed by the habitual feelings associated with our various experiences—feelings of lack, bitterness, and soul-longing. I do not suggest living in a delusional state of absurdly ecstatic and abnormal emotions, nor do I advocate clinging constantly to a single feeling; that would neither be feasible nor desirable. However, the prevailing feeling within us should be one of joy and gratitude for the privilege of possessing this marvelous conscious existence.

But what about those whose consciousness renders unconsciousness preferable? How can they rejoice in possessing such consciousness—feeling cold, hungry, unloved, uneducated, and seemingly ensnared in a web of adverse circumstances from which escape appears impossible?

Every normal human being harbors within themselves certain powers that enable them to transcend any condition and attain any state. They may not know how to wield these powers, but they possess them nonetheless. Numerous instances attest to this, where seemingly insurmountable changes have occurred, lifting the unfortunate out of despair into conditions beyond their wildest imaginings. While some may attribute these occurrences to chance or luck, they are, in fact, the result of forces acting in accordance with immutable laws, whether or not we comprehend those actions. Our ignorance of the intricate workings of our bodies and the forces we command keeps us bound to unhappy conditions.

The power of feeling has long been underestimated and relegated to a secondary role in our lives. Throughout history, we've endured tortures and lived in fear, with suffering preached as a pathway to happiness in the afterlife, stifling our innate joy in living. However, feeling is a potent force that is just beginning to be understood. We are realizing that there is nothing virtuous in misery; on the contrary, it is a sin to be miserable and a virtue to be happy.

This great power we possess is threefold, and our will, intellect, and feeling must each play a role in governing our lives. Merely willing our conditions to align with our desires is futile unless our thoughts and feelings align with that intention. When we train ourselves to do so, we will experience the true Joy of Living.

If our thoughts and feelings are rebellious, if we view life as a burden and our bodies as troublesome encumbrances, merely exerting our will exhausts the nervous system in a fruitless attempt to accomplish alone what thought and feeling should be aiding, rather than opposing.

I once observed two brakemen on a passenger train, and their contrasting approaches to their duties were quite evident. One was alert, active, with a beaming face radiating the joy of living; the other performed his tasks begrudgingly, sullenly, and with visible reluctance. If he was dissatisfied with his work and sought a more fulfilling occupation, he wasn't taking the right approach to attain it. Until we can perform our responsibilities well and cheerfully, we don't deserve anything better, and even if we had it, we wouldn't find satisfaction.

We must rise above undesirable conditions internally before we can do so externally. We must train our thoughts and feelings to reject any consciousness of unhappiness and instead embrace the joy of living. We must sever ties with despondency, irritation, and dissatisfaction, and wholeheartedly embrace the joy of existence before we can attract happier conditions to ourselves.

We must tap into our inner reservoirs of strength to the extent that petty annoyances and unsuitable environments lose their significance, serving only as opportunities to test our capabilities. Once we have mastered control over our inner forces, changes in our external lives will follow. However, cultivating this habitual mental attitude is the initial step in managing external circumstances. We cannot expect to be strong outwardly until we are strong internally, and we cannot achieve inner strength while allowing spite, jealousy, unkindness, or trouble to diminish the joy of living that rightfully belongs to us and becomes an indomitable power once firmly entrenched in our hearts.

Recently, I came across a quote by Charles Wagner that encapsulates a profound truth: "Joy is a sacred flame which must be fed and which throws a splendid radiance over life." This flame resides within all of our hearts. If it flickers low, we must fan it into a brighter and brighter glow until it banishes every dark and fearful corner.

If we desire to illuminate our lives with this "splendid radiance," we must render ourselves impervious to the ill-natured attitudes of those around us, so that petty jealousies and unkindnesses leave no mark on our spirits. As for harboring such feelings within ourselves, that is out of the question if we aim to elevate ourselves into happy circumstances and congenial surroundings.

It is folly to expect to grow in happiness and prosperity while harboring spiteful and jealous feelings toward those who are happy and successful. This mindset reflects weakness that must be overcome before we can achieve our desired outcomes.

We must not postpone happiness until circumstances align with our desires. We must commence being happy right now and persist in our happiness despite everything, while also taking every feasible action to manifest our desired conditions.

We don't have to wait long before noticing improvements when we earnestly endeavor to stoke the flame of joy within our hearts. Among the people we know who are miserable and discontented, a vast majority create their troubles by dwelling on and magnifying their difficulties.

The happiness or misery in our lives isn't determined by the actions, words, or thoughts of others but by our inner state. When we habitually think and feel that everything is working together for our good, maintaining that state of consciousness effortlessly, the flame of joy burns so brightly within us that no darkness can dim its "splendid radiance."

We must not allow a single harsh or bitter thought to linger within us. If we cannot elevate ourselves above unkind feelings, we lack the necessary strength to progress further. We must begin at the outset—and the outset is the right mental attitude. All the vexing things others say or do must roll off our consciousness like water off a good roof; not a drop should seep through to disrupt the harmony of our inner lives.

It is crucial to remember: It isn't the best general who engages in the most fighting. When our focus is on happy conditions, petty annoyances and overwhelming sorrows lose their power to drag us into despondency. It is a misconception to believe that the path to happiness is rugged and thorny, as we've been taught.

The Meaning of Life

Life holds different meanings for each individual. From its vast storehouse of treasures, everyone seeks what brings them happiness. Some give up early in the struggle, content with mere existence, never delving deeply into life's mysteries. Others waste their energies chasing superficial trappings that do not truly bring happiness, blinded by their flashy allure.

Some have access to secret chambers where power and riches await those who possess the key. Some are crushed in senseless pursuits of unworthy objects, while others perish striving for something of immeasurable value. Yet, their efforts often draw attention to what they sought, and their successors succeed where they failed. These individuals have not toiled in vain; though they may not have unearthed the treasures they sought, they have revealed their existence to the world.

Often, we accumulate treasures not just for ourselves but for future generations. If our labor were solely for ourselves, there would be little motivation for effort. We truly live when we are aware that we are ever-changing expressions of universal power, inseparable from the great universe.

In working for posterity, we work for ourselves. By bringing forth hidden treasures to enrich the world, we make it a happier place for humanity. We, as indestructible elements of nature, shall reap what we sow and share the fruits of our efforts with future generations.

Life's storehouse is filled with wonders: unexplored passages, mysterious towers with unopened doors, and dungeons holding secrets best left buried. There are steep stairways that the faint-hearted avoid but reward patient climbers with chambers filled with rare treasures. Truly, "Not half of the joys that await them to mortals has ever been told."

It is a grand privilege to partake in life's rich possessions, to receive the invitation to "Knock, and it shall be opened unto you," to "Seek and ye shall find." Yet, despite this wealth at our disposal, why are we often lacking in mental and material possessions? The answer is simple: we do not know how to harness our inherent powers, or if we do, we fail to apply that knowledge. The world is slowly awakening to these hidden powers, but it still wonders if it is all just a dream.

We are gradually realizing that the material world is a visible expression of the mental world in which we truly reside and where our greatest powers of achievement lie. We cannot attract happiness by carrying ourselves with downcast looks and aching hearts, clinging to our griefs and dwelling upon them from a mistaken sense of duty.

On the contrary, if we confront fate boldly and fearlessly, laughing at the frowning look she directs at us, we shall find her laughing back at us. A happy person radiates happiness, which returns with interest. It's important to remember that happiness will go out of its way to avoid a dismal countenance. Therefore, if we wish to be happy, we must simply feel happy, regardless of how dismal the outlook may seem. If we can confidently affirm, "It is well with my soul," and steadfastly hold onto that feeling, troubles will vanish before it, as if by magic.

It is foolish to believe that the happiness of our lives has passed and to linger nostalgically in the flowery paths of the past. By looking forward with hopeful hearts, we will discover, as we progress, undreamed-of joys and marvelous manifestations of a power that always leads the willing follower into paths where new delights await. One should never consider themselves too old or unfortunate to have friends to love and to stay connected with the world in which we live.

While our consciousness expands to comprehend the hidden powers of the universe more broadly, we are not departing from materialism. Instead, we are taking materialism with us into this realm of subtle power, for there is nothing more mysterious than the material part of the universe, itself a manifestation of active energy of inconceivable power. Our soul powers are no more mysterious and awe-inspiring than our bodies, those marvelous instruments upon which external forces are constantly acting, "As when on harp Æolian, Zephyr plays."

Life offers us grand opportunities by granting us these remarkable mental and physical powers, although many of us find ourselves in the position of the boy who won an elephant in the lottery and didn't know what to do with it. However, just as we learned to walk by walking, despite bumps and tumbles, we learn to live by living itself, gradually mastering the art of using the powers in our possession. There is no art more fascinating or worthy of cultivation.

"The proper study of mankind is man." But when man begins to study himself, he realizes that he must reach far beyond what he previously considered himself to be. He is not merely a soul and body bound together for a time, but, I repeat, an ever-changing expression of universal power.

The Power of Love

Love is a word that has been long-suffering and much abused. Its meaning varies greatly depending on the understanding of the individual. To the Christian, it represents the love of God for a sin-blighted world, leading Him to sacrifice His only Son to lift the burden of sin from it. For many, it symbolizes a universal power always ready to lift a sin-weary and sin-cursed people into the heaven of purity and happiness, surrounding them if they choose to attract it.

To a doting parent, it implies unselfish devotion to an adored child; to the loving child, it means a clinging fondness for one providing protection and adoration; to the brother, friend, or neighbor, it carries yet another meaning; while to the lover, it can signify anything from a sentimental fancy to the "Grand Passion."

Love is an "old story ever new." Birds have sung it, winds have whispered it, and poets have sung of it in various melodies since the dawn of life. Some lament, "What is love, but repining?"Others mourn, "The falcon has the eyes of the dove. Ah, Love! Perjured, false, treacherous Love! Enemy of all that mankind may not rue! Most untrue To him who keeps most faith with thee!"

While others sing cheerfully, "Beauty lies In many eyes; But love in yours, my Nora Creina!" and "Oh, 'tis love, 'tis love, 'tis love, That makes the world go round!"

Each appeal resonates differently with each reader based on their experiences and understanding; some may discard the book and wonder what these poets are raving about. Speaking of poets, the unknown author of the "Song of Solomon," a love poem intertwined with the Bible, surpassed modern poets in expressing the power of love and revealed a deep understanding of its meaning when he said, "For love is strong as death."

"Great waters cannot quench love, and rivers cannot overwhelm it."

"If a man would offer all his substance for love, He would only reap confusion."

These truths about genuine love remain as valid today as they were three thousand years ago when written, and will endure three thousand years hence, for truth transcends eternity.

The most delightful aspect of love is that money cannot purchase it. It must be given freely or not at all. Even the poorest beggar who has experienced the strength of this remarkable power would not trade it for all the wealth of the world. "For love is strong as death."

Yet, love's power is entirely for happiness, life, and light. Selfishness plays no part in love, as the self is wholly absorbed in the object of adoration. The willingness to die for a loved one is not an empty or exaggerated assertion. Many have sacrificed their lives to save strangers, while true love would instinctively place itself between a loved one and any threat.

Love recognizes no sacrifice too great if it enhances the happiness of the beloved. Even jealousy, that "green-eyed monster," is subdued by the influence of genuine, unselfish love. "For love is strong as death."

It is the vilest slander to attribute to love the atrocities for which it is sometimes held responsible. The individual who resorts to violence in the name of love is a blatant impostor. Such actions are not motivated by love but rather by irrational hatred and selfishness.

Love never advocates violence or dishonor. To do so would be to invite its own demise, for love cannot thrive in such an environment. Hatred and jealousy are love's sworn enemies, constantly seeking to destroy what love builds. Their power is for evil, while love's power is for good. Love is a facet of the soul's power, a life-giving force that purifies and strengthens the blood, much like happy and wholesome thoughts affect the brain's gray matter.

Love is the finest of medicines, while thoughts and feelings of hatred and anger inevitably harm the body's well-being.

There is perhaps no sight more sorrowful than a person devoid of love. Animals exhibit this soul-power remarkably, exemplified by the dog that lovingly licks the hand of its abusive master, displaying a nobility and contentment surpassing that of the master. While humans may not possess the same capacity to love the unlovable, they can always find something deserving of their affection and refrain from harboring hatred towards that which repels them.

Love has the power to rejuvenate a faded complexion, revive the sparkle in a dull eye, infuse energy into weary steps, and bring joy to a grieving heart. It has the ability to shape the fate of nations, conquer animosity and rage, thwart spite and malice, cast a radiant aura upon even the humblest circumstances of life, and fashion a paradise amidst earthly struggles.

A Happy Consciousness

Someone once remarked that without life, the universe would be wasted; however, without consciousness, life itself would be squandered.

A joyful consciousness stands as the pinnacle achievement of nature's endeavors. A joyful consciousness! It represents the fundamental aim behind all the marvels witnessed throughout the ages. The antiquated notion that "Man was made to mourn" is being consigned to the dustbin of history, alongside other outdated rhetoric ill-suited to modern ethical sensibilities. Man was not fashioned for perpetual sorrow; rather, he was intended to gaze optimistically towards the future, instead of languishing in despondency over the past. To assert that there is no hope is absurd. Hope persists eternally—"while there is life."

The enduring adage that "Hope springs eternal in the human breast" serves as evidence that hope is not without justification. Surely, nature would not instill this sweet hope within us if there were not valid reasons to hope, nor would it implant within man a soul-stirring desire without providing the means to fulfill it. Yet, man must actively seek out these means; he must pursue the truth independently, and if he earnestly endeavors, assistance will be forthcoming, for God cannot aid man unless he takes steps to help himself.

As he begins to aid himself by making efforts within his limited capacity, he will find assistance as he progresses—aid that arrives unexpectedly and when needed.

Disasters are inevitable; storms beset both the psyche and the physical realm. However, there is purpose in the intensity of feeling aroused by such mental upheavals. They serve to prepare the soul for the happiness that follows. "The darkest hour is just before the dawn."

Consciousness cannot remain in a perpetual state of happiness, as its very existence depends on change. Thomas Moore eloquently captured this truth, stating:

"We've had some happy hours together,
But joy must often change its wing;
And spring would be but gloomy weather
If we had nothing else but spring."

Consciousness has aptly been described as the window of the mind, through which it gazes outward and communicates with kindred minds, perceiving the works of its hand. Like will, thought, and feeling, consciousness serves as an instrument of Mind, which we can only define as that which we are conscious of being, and which we recognize in connection with everything in nature.

Consciousness embodies the sum of the soul's powers. To be conscious is to know, but we cannot know without feeling, and we cannot feel without knowing. Our understanding may be limited, but we are at least aware that we experience feelings, and to feel and know is to will. Even an infant knows that it feels, as evidenced by its hearty cries demanding that those feelings be pleasant.

We feel, we know, we will. To that extent, we are conscious, and this consciousness of knowing, feeling, and willing arises from rates of motion stimulated in the brain's cells. These rates may be conveyed to the brain cells by certain nerves (afferent), with optic nerve impulses resulting in the consciousness of light and auditory nerve impulses leading to the recognition of sound. We say, "I hear," to denote this state of consciousness. Sensations vary depending on the differences in rates of motion conveyed to the brain cells by the afferent nerves, known as afferent stimuli.

However, not all these rates result from stimuli external to the body, such as light and sound. Within the body, there are nerve centers that transmit impulses to the brain cells, differing from sensory impulses induced by ether and air waves.

Thus, we are aware of forces operating not only outside the body but also within it. The recognition that our nerve centers serve as hubs of force has led to much speculation about our latent powers, occult forces, and so forth. The inner forces, which are currently the subject of much discussion, are no more enigmatic or "occult" than the external forces surrounding us.

Over the ages, the mind has managed to develop an organism that boasts a high level of consciousness by arranging matter differently, resulting in varying rates of motion and the ability to convert the forms of energy derived from these rates into other forms of energy.

Prior to the addition of higher brain centers in vertebrates, the spinal nerve centers only offered a rudimentary level of consciousness, limited to mere recognition of existence and immediate surroundings.

It seems scarcely believable that anyone would seriously argue that if we were not conscious, there would be nothing to be conscious of—that everything exists only as a state of consciousness. Yet, such assertions have been made earnestly. Forces would continue to operate in nature even without consciousness, which is merely the outcome of the rates of motion these forces elicit in the brain cells, rates that can only be received through the action of nerves and blood, as the brain itself "may be cut, burned, or electrified, without producing pain."

The functioning of blood in the brain is essential for consciousness; its sudden withdrawal induces a fainting spell and temporarily suspends consciousness.

Personality represents the degree of consciousness commanded by the bodily organism. Thoughts come and go, leaving an indelible mark of their presence on the grey nerve-matter of the brain. Sustaining a single state of consciousness for long is not feasible. Should the will allow the continuous recurrence of one thought or stream of thoughts, the brain becomes "unbalanced." A change occurs in the brain, leading to a change in personality. Thought constantly molds the brain and, consequently, the personality. Hence, we are the architects of our own characters. We must think. While the will cannot halt the force we call thought, it can steer and utilize it to cultivate desired conditions.

The assertion that we are never fully conscious is intriguing and warrants contemplation. We feel—we know—we will. To that extent, we are conscious. However, have we harnessed these powers to their fullest potential?

No two personalities are identical because no two individuals can harbor precisely the same thoughts, feelings, and will, and thus cannot experience consciousness to exactly the same degree. Furthermore, no person remains in a constant state or level of consciousness for long. Growth in knowledge, acquired through experience, is indispensable for our existence. The old adage, "Live and learn," succinctly captures this reality.

However, the wisdom possessed by even the wisest individual pales in comparison to that which remains beyond their grasp. We have scant insight into the thoughts and feelings of those around us, often inadvertently causing hurt to our loved ones.

The underutilization of the will is a glaring reality, and the power of feelings is seldom acknowledged for what it truly is—a potent force that must be reckoned with.

For years, we may trudge along in a monotonous manner, unaware of the depth of our emotions until some seemingly random set of circumstances awakens us to feelings previously unexplored. These emotions allow us to better understand the poet's words:

"There are depths of love that we cannot know,
Till we cross the narrow sea.
There are heights of joy that we may not reach,
Till we rest in peace with Thee."

Psychologists recognize the existence of a conscious state separate from waking consciousness but intimately connected to it—the subconscious mind. While superior in consciousness, it is subservient to the will of the waking consciousness and plays a significant role in achieving its objectives. This mysterious "subconscious mentality" bears a strong resemblance to Habit in many respects.

While we sleep, the subconscious mind acts upon the suggestions received from our waking thoughts. Hence, it is essential to ensure that our thoughts as we fall asleep are positive and constructive. If filled with love, happiness, and hope, the subconscious mind employs its mystic power to manifest favorable conditions around us. If initial efforts fail, we must persist, as failures often pave the way for success.

Despair should not grip us if happiness eludes us initially or arrives through unexpected means. We must trust fate to orchestrate the manner of its fulfillment while focusing on our immediate duties, however trivial they may seem. Fate is more than capable of fulfilling its part of the bargain.

Conversely, falling asleep with thoughts and feelings of pride, coldness, or aloofness erects barriers between us and others, fostering loneliness and isolation. No success is worthwhile if it lacks love and happiness.

On the other hand, going to sleep with a mind burdened by care, anxiety, or negativity sets powerful forces in motion that perpetuate misery until a psychical storm, spurred by rebellious feelings, brings relief, albeit sometimes through hardship.

Brooding over past suffering or the misfortune of others is a grievous sin, devoid of any virtue and utterly pernicious. It yields no happiness and serves as an intolerable nuisance. A happy consciousness is the ultimate purpose of life, the rightful inheritance of every living being.

Necessity of Change

Change is an inherent aspect of existence. It is the toll we pay for the gift of consciousness, the precious jewel for which nature sets the stage. From the moment we draw our first breath to the seeming finality of our last, our lives are a continuous series of transformations marking our growth. This development persists beyond what is conventionally termed maturity, for we continue to mature as long as we live.

There is purpose in aging, just as there is in youth. Age offers opportunities unimagined by those who view it solely as a wearisome wait for death. It's crucial to remember that the soul never ages. It is only when we lose interest in life that we invite dissolution, for change is inevitable. If we fail to harness the forces we embody, we become easy prey to the destructive elements of nature.

Some elderly individuals have allowed their disappointments to embitter their lives, harboring only hatred and jealousy towards the young and more fortunate. They overlook the fact that the young also face their own trials and tribulations, which can be just as burdensome, whether real or imagined. "Deal gently with the old, for they have traveled far, and be kind to the young, for they have a long journey ahead." I do not know the originator of this excellent advice, but it encapsulates a beautiful sentiment.

There are delightful elderly individuals who have maintained youthful and hopeful hearts despite the changes and disappointments of passing years—men and women who are charming companions for the young and old alike. It's not always those with the most trying experiences who harbor bitterness; more often, it's those who live solely for themselves and miss out on the joy of living.

The vitality of every cell in our bodies hinges on constant exchange—giving and receiving, expelling waste and replenishing with new material. Similarly, our lives should embody a cycle of giving and receiving. As we give our best to the world, we receive in return. Just as active cells grow stronger, our lives are enriched and invigorated when we adhere to the law of reciprocity.

Some may argue that they give without receiving, but this suggests an unwise mode of giving. Those who give wisely always receive, if not immediately, then eventually. Conversely, there are those who give nothing yet lament their lack of receiving, and others who seem to receive much without giving. However, they often pay a hefty price in the end.

Activity is the cornerstone of life; stagnation leads to death, paving the way for new activities of a different nature. Just as water vapor rises from the ocean, condenses in colder air, and falls back to earth, perpetuating the cycle, so do we undergo changes. It's unrealistic to expect enduring circumstances; thus, it's prudent to recognize the transient nature of things and seize the opportunities change presents.

Opportunity may knock but once, but it is never far from us. If we earnestly seek it, we will find it. If opportunity doesn't come to us, we must pursue it. Our lives would be brighter and happier if we embraced change. Nature did not intend for us to lead dull, monotonous lives. Like food and clothing, change is essential for us to be at our best and make the most of our lives.

Sometimes we welcome change, while at other times, we rebel against what we deem undesirable, questioning nature's wisdom with bitterness. Conditions are ever-evolving—mighty individuals fall, the lowly rise, cities vanish, inventions revolutionize, and life and death collaborate to sustain the perpetual change nature demands.

Energy is always at work, and the wondrous displays of power we witness are the outcomes of energy's transformations. Modern wonders like the telephone exemplify how energy can be converted from one form to another to enhance our existence.

Reflecting on the changes of our lives, we are astounded by the transformations that have made life today vastly different from that of our forebears. We cannot predict the future or anticipate its changes. Instead, we must greet the ever-moving, ever-changing current of life with cheerful hearts as it propels us towards the boundless expanse of the future.

All is fleeting. It is the indispensable condition through which we experience conscious existence.

The Evils of Fear

The detrimental effects of fear cannot be overstated. It's regrettable that we've been taught to believe that living in "the fear of the Lord"—not to mention fearing "the world, the flesh, and the devil"—is virtuous.

The practice of using fear of punishment to compel children to behave is increasingly viewed unfavorably. Those in positions to influence the training of children are seriously considering how best to address this issue. The challenge of nurturing a child's best qualities while eliminating undesirable traits is complex, but instilling fear in anyone's mind is hardly a desirable solution.

Fear, whether it's the threat of punishment for a misbehaving child or the specter of eternal damnation, has never truly made anyone morally upright or diminished their inherent evil. Even those who profess belief in eternal punishment for others often expect to evade such consequences themselves.

Speculation about the afterlife—such as how the wicked will be punished and the virtuous rewarded—often arises from the perceived injustices and unpunished crimes in this life. However, the concept of endless torture after death serves neither justice nor reformation. It harkens back to a time of barbarism when torture and execution were common.

While remnants of such brutality persist, there are hopeful signs, such as the Emmanuel movement, which focuses on addressing sin and suffering in the present. It emphasizes the importance of understanding and utilizing natural forces to uplift humanity here and now, rather than relying on vague notions of supernatural existence.

It's fortunate that virtue is its own reward, as endless torture after death could never be considered just. Such an idea is reminiscent of the barbaric practices of the past, which have thankfully diminished over time.

Despite progress, instances of savagery still occur, as evidenced by the disturbing sentiments expressed by a retired clergyman advocating violence against heretics and blasphemers. Such attitudes are incompatible with the teachings of compassion and forgiveness attributed to Jesus.

In conclusion, fear should not be used as a tool to enforce obedience or suppress dissent. Instead, society should strive to cultivate empathy, understanding, and respect for all individuals, regardless of their beliefs or actions.

There can be no greater blasphemy than what is expressed in the preceding words. Even though the person making such statements might refuse to acknowledge it as such, their words brim with savagery and lack any trace of Christian values. It resembles the war cries of a savage brandishing a tomahawk over their victim, incapable of bringing about any greater good.

In contrast, the Emmanuel movement represents a beacon of hope in addressing the issues of sin and suffering. It emphasizes action in the present to uplift those suffering from forces they do not comprehend. Rather than relying on vague notions of an afterlife, whether heavenly or hellish, it focuses on improving conditions here and now.

When the root causes of crime, misery, and disease are addressed, there will be less need for extreme measures like execution. Engaging in violence and destruction only leads to further cycles of crime, ignorance, and misery.

Comparing the Emmanuel movement to the bloodthirsty nature of certain religions, it's evident which offers more promise for uplifting humanity.

It's high time for the church to acknowledge and teach the profound truth that "God is with us." Ignorance of this fact has led us to conflict and strife, perpetually losing ourselves in futile attempts to save our lives.

When we grasp that we are greater than any external circumstances and that we are the masters of our own fate, fear loses its grip on us. We need not fear our own potential for harm when we understand how to harness the powerful forces within us for good.

Hope serves as the antidote to fear, illuminating our path and dispelling the shadows of doubt and insecurity that plague us. We must reject the habit of fear and embrace a hopeful outlook filled with joy and certainty that all will be well.

The Secret of Power

The secret to attaining power lies in overcoming obstacles—these obstacles need not be monumental, but merely ones that impede further progress. "An obstacle is something not to be shirked, but to be overcome."

The true significance of the promise, "To him that overcometh I will give a crown of life," has often been misconstrued. The attainment of power inevitably follows overcoming, as it is a fundamental law of nature.

Power denotes the ability to surmount resistance, and it invariably seeks expression in this manner. We enhance our power by utilizing whatever resources we possess. Even if initially meager, once we employ them to overcome a challenge, we gain in power, making it easier to conquer subsequent obstacles. Progress becomes possible when we take the first step. I wish I could emphasize this point strongly enough for its truth and significance to resonate with everyone who reads these words. We can always advance toward any goal or desire when we initiate action.

It is erroneous to believe that engaging in seemingly trivial pursuits signifies wasting our lives. Many of us lack a clear vision of a specific goal we are striving towards. However, it is essential to reach an understanding with ourselves and identify what we truly desire. This marks the initial step. The subsequent step involves overcoming any obstacle in our path, regardless of how minor it may seem. Through this act of overcoming, however insignificant, we gain power. Once we make this beginning, progress becomes feasible. It is through conquering minor obstacles that we accumulate the strength to surmount major challenges.

Just as our physical strength grows with disciplined exercise, the same principle applies to our spiritual faculties, which are equally natural and subject to natural laws. To enhance our physical strength, we diligently care for our bodies and engage in exercises that develop their capabilities.

However, we possess a power that transcends mere physical strength—soul power. While similar to mechanical energy, soul power is distinct in its form and potency. Like electricity, it is invisible yet real. Every sensation and emotion we experience is a manifestation of this power. Soul power, though intangible, is as tangible as electricity. The misuse of these inner forces, akin to the ignorant use of electricity, can have devastating consequences.

These soul powers are intricately linked with the body, and their efficacy is influenced by its condition. The depths of soul power remain unfathomable, for as we utilize the power at our disposal, more is bestowed upon us. The body indeed serves as the vessel for the divine.

To acquire power, we must commence by overcoming something, no matter how trivial—a habitual thought pattern, unkind speech, or a physical gesture. Each victory, however minor, augments our power, propelling us forward with increasing momentum. With newfound confidence and strength, we can persistently pursue our heart's desires, surmounting any obstacles that lie in our path.

It is imperative to have a lofty purpose or goal, take the initial step, and persistently advance towards success, overcoming obstacles along the way. Through this continual process of overcoming, we steadily accumulate power until we possess the strength to conquer even the most formidable challenges. Along this journey, we not only experience the joy of progress but also the satisfaction of overcoming.

The law of progression underpins our restlessness and innate desire for continual advancement. Scholars seek greater knowledge, magnates desire more wealth, and artists strive for greater mastery. We all recognize that beyond what we currently possess, lies an infinite reservoir of potential.

We utilize only a portion of our brain cells, leading to speculation about the purpose of the surplus cells. It's apparent that in the process of evolving organisms with heightened consciousness, Nature has ensured an ample supply of brain cells to accommodate increasing levels of thought. In lower animals, the number of higher brain cells is limited but expands with evolutionary development. Although these surplus brain cells may seem superfluous, they signify the potential for higher levels of organization that evolution is gradually shaping.

A cell isn't merely a repository for thoughts like a bee's honeycomb or a jailer's prison. It's a living entity, a mass of protoplasm containing a central nucleus with remarkable capabilities. In multi-cellular organisms, such as plants or animals, various types of cells form different tissues within the body. Our entire bodily structure is composed of these living cells.

With such an extraordinary organism, there's no need to fear aspiring to any desire or reaching the limits of knowledge or power. Eternity is guaranteed because energy is indestructible and perpetually engaged in work. The conclusion of one endeavor marks the inception of another. We shouldn't despair when faced with failure; there's always a future opportunity to achieve success, even if we've made repeated mistakes. Success lies not in avoiding mistakes altogether but in learning from them and not repeating them. Even if we've made the same mistake numerous times, success is still attainable through earnest effort and the right approach. The right approach is singular: to acquire the power to overcome significant challenges, we must commence at the beginning and develop strength incrementally as we progress.

Mind and Matter

The human mind is likened to a small spark of the universal mind, evident in all natural activities. Even will, though supreme, relies on the guiding power of mind. Mind operates according to unchanging principles, with Habit being chief among them. While the grand plan of the universe may be beyond our full comprehension, we can be certain of its goodness. As beings with conscious existence, we possess the privilege to ignite the flames of love and enthusiasm wherever needed to elevate humanity toward a happier state—an integral part of the grand plan with which we are intimately involved.

It's difficult to conceive of mind without matter; even if invisible, it exists in some form of substance. Matter, defined as that which occupies space, encompasses ether, which fills the spaces between atoms and particles. Luminiferous ether, the medium through which light and heat propagate, is considered the ultimate substance from which all else emanates and returns. While its composition remains unknown, it's undeniable that ether must exist to facilitate the transmission of energy.

As matter is a result of various rates of motion, and forces stem from different modes of motion, it's reasonable to conclude that ether also arises from motion beyond our current understanding. The theory of soul-bodies composed of psychomeres parallels our material bodies being made of electrons, suggesting that ether has a similar composition—a unit rate of motion corresponding to the material atom.

Every manifestation of energy is a manifestation of mind, leading some to equate mind and energy. Each cell possesses its own form of intelligence, contributing to the body's functions. Even when individual consciousness ceases, the mind continues to operate within the fixed conditions of sustaining life, governed by the law of Habit.

The example of a pigeon, which acts mechanically without consciousness after the removal of its cerebrum, illustrates the power of Habit in guiding nerve center responses to stimuli. While there's no conscious purpose behind the pigeon's actions, there's purpose in the application of the law of Habit governing its behavior.

Instinct serves as evidence of mind, yet instinctual acts are as mechanical as the movements of the pigeon previously mentioned. They result from habits ingrained in the organism across generations, guiding nerve centers to respond to specific stimuli and produce fixed outcomes.

Bees demonstrate remarkable feats in comb-building, honey-making, and governance, all driven by habit. The intricate construction of a honeycomb involves complex mathematical principles beyond human comprehension. While bees don't calculate these formulas consciously, it's evident that the same universal mind governing physiological functions also orchestrates their intricate work.

A human body may possess physical beauty, but without a beautiful mind, its charm fades. Mind is the essence that imbues physical life with meaning, shaping our soul-life—the true essence of existence. A charming personality stems from an interesting and balanced mind, attuned to nature and complementing physical abilities.

Mind serves as the counselor of will and feeling, though feeling can sometimes offer superior guidance. High character lies in discerning when feeling should take precedence. Charles Dickens' portrayal of Little Sissy Jupe in "Hard Times" highlights the folly of prioritizing rigid reason over tender human emotions.

Feeling, an essential aspect of the soul, should be nurtured and integrated into intellectual and volitional deliberations.

The potential of the human mind knows few bounds. In our brief lifetimes, we accumulate knowledge from generations past and contribute to the enrichment of future minds. However, what constitutes knowledge evolves over time, with today's truths often debunked by tomorrow's science. Human thought perpetually quests for truth, driving philosophical inquiry.

An old textbook on Intellectual Philosophy by Hubbard Winslow reflects the progress of the past fifty years. While some facts remain timeless, others fall into obscurity as knowledge advances. The text's description of intense mental activity in moments of bodily incapacity raises profound questions about the mind's independence from the body—a topic still debated by contemporary scholars.

Whether the mind or soul can separate from the physical body during coma, sleep, or death remains a subject of serious discussion among eminent scholars. While opinions vary, humanity's growing understanding of the mind-body relationship promises intriguing developments. Yet, definitive answers to these age-old questions may elude us for some time, as the nature of mind and matter continues to captivate human inquiry.

Waves, Tides, and Currents

It is notable that in exploring the causes behind natural phenomena, we consistently encounter wave motion. From the ripple of a thought to the tremor of an earthquake, wave motion is ever-present. It's reassuring that the supreme intelligence responsible for these extraordinary displays of power has provided visible and tangible examples of the invisible and intangible, enabling us to grasp what would otherwise be incomprehensible.

In the movement of water waves, we find a parallel to the invisible ether waves, whose rates of motion give rise to various forms of energy, as well as the waves traversing the solid yet elastic portions of the earth's surface.

Recent scientific findings align with a theory I previously posited without authority. It appears that the same gravitational attraction causing tidal waves in the liquid portion of the earth also generates similar waves in the solid, albeit less yielding, portion. Recent observations confirm that the earth's surface does indeed undergo fluctuations, a natural expectation rather than a surprise.

The universal law of gravitation dictates that every particle of matter attracts every other particle to some extent. This attractive force, known as gravitation, operates akin to pulling a heavy weight toward oneself with a slender thread. The gravitational pull varies with distance and quantity of the attracting bodies. The moon and sun, being closest to the earth, exert significant gravitational influence, giving rise to tides both in water and the earth's crust.

Tides, circling the earth as the moon orbits it, reach their highest points when the gravitational forces of the moon and sun align. Tidal waves and earthquakes likely result from gravitational stresses, as the positions of celestial bodies constantly shift, causing their gravitational pull to exert strains on both water and the earth's crust. This strain intensifies when the waves from different bodies reinforce each other, combining their crests to produce greater effects.

The phenomenon of the earth's surface rising and falling with a significant tide every twelve hours, as reported by Camille Flammarion and German savant Hecker, is not incredulous. What's astonishing is the oversight by scholars who failed to recognize the necessity of such actions on an elastic substance under the influence of gravitational forces, similar to the effects observed in water.

There is a striking similarity between tidal waves and powerful earthquake waves. Both impact the deepest parts of the sea, and their velocity increases with the depth of the water. For instance, the great earthquake waves from Arica, Peru, in 1868 traveled thousands of miles at astonishing speeds, demonstrating the profound effects of such waves.

The planets can be envisioned as immersed in a vast sea of ether, with every vibrating particle imparting motion to this ether. This motion is then transmitted to other planets, with varying effects depending on distance and speed. The light we perceive, traveling at incredible speeds, originates from vibrations set in motion ages ago, illustrating the vastness of the universe and its temporal scales.

Given the perpetual movement of planets and their changing gravitational relationships, it's plausible that celestial bodies influence our lives. While I don't refer to astrology in the sense of fortune-telling, the gravitational interactions among celestial bodies may indeed impact terrestrial events. Just as there are tides in the earth, air, and water, there might be metaphorical tides in our lives, influenced by cosmic forces.

In times of adversity, it's often said that when everything seems bleak, that's precisely when fortunes may change. However, it's essential not only to persevere but also to discern when to let go and allow the tide to carry us toward better circumstances. Beyond our individual efforts, there seems to be a greater force at play, often referred to as Fate or Divine Providence, shaping the course of our lives.

Human existence unfolds amidst a sea of ether and air waves, impacting us on various levels—physically, emotionally, and spiritually. We emit and receive waves of thought, feeling, and energy, shaping our experiences and interactions. It's crucial to be mindful of the waves we generate and attract, ensuring they align with our well-being and aspirations.

Life and soul-powers, once considered mystical or beyond human comprehension, are now viewed more rationally as integral aspects of our existence. While unraveling the mysteries of human nature may take time, adopting a naturalistic perspective offers insights into our complexities and potential.

Just as there are currents in the oceans and air, there may be metaphorical currents in our lives—some propelling us toward success and happiness, others dragging us into despair. Understanding how to navigate these currents, through positive habits of thought and action, is key to realizing our aspirations and fulfilling our potential.

☯☯☯

Energy and Motion

The diversity of energy forms arises from varying rates of motion, with all natural phenomena stemming from these rates and the conversion of energy from one form to another. Although it's the same energy at its core, different rates of motion yield different effects or manifestations that we perceive.

Matter itself emerges from the motion rates of corpuscles or electrons within atoms. These electrons orbit each other at tremendous speeds, primarily consisting of positive and negative electric charges—hence they are termed electrons. The atom, considered the smallest unit of matter, results from the motion rates of these electrons. Matter, broadly defined as that which occupies space, includes both individual electrons and the ether filling the spaces between them. The understanding of matter has expanded with advancements in physical science, notably recognizing its electrical foundation due to the divisibility of the atom.

Electricity, like sound, light, and heat, also arises from specific rates of motion. These energy forms are effects produced when motion rates propagate in waves through elastic mediums like air or ether, interacting with other matter. The resulting wave motion can be traced back to vibrating particles of matter, with the waves inducing similar vibrations in other bodies upon impact. When these waves interact with our bodies, they stimulate nerve cells, which convey the motion rates to the brain. Consciousness emerges as a result of these motion rates exciting nerve matter in the brain. As long as we are conscious, the brain vibrates in response to pulsations from blood cells and nerve fibers.

Until around the year 1840, heat was commonly perceived as a fluid permeating matter, akin to air or ether. However, it is now understood that heat arises from the motion of molecules within a substance, with the intensity of heat corresponding to the degree of molecular agitation. Cold, therefore, is simply a lower degree of heat. Even in what we perceive as a cold stove, the molecules are in motion, albeit at a slower rate than when heated. Heat, like light, propagates through ether rather than air, with the only distinction being in wavelength.

As ether permeates all matter, akin to water surrounding a fish, the motion of vibrating molecules induces wave motion in ether. These waves radiate from the vibrating mass of matter, creating a sphere of ether waves around it. When these waves encounter our bodies, they excite molecular activity, modulated by the medium through which they pass. This is how we receive heat (and light) from the sun. Notably, it is not heat itself that travels but rather the wave motion induced by heat, capable of stimulating motion rates in bodies, which we perceive as heat.

Unlike heat and light, sound requires a denser medium. Sound waves cannot propagate in a vacuum; rather, they are induced by vibrating particles of matter in air or any other denser elastic substance. When these waves reach the ear, they cause vibrations in the auditory nerve, which transmit the motion rates to the brain, resulting in the perception of sound. However, before reaching the brain, these pulsations are modified by the medium they pass through.

Some philosophers argue that all external phenomena exist only in consciousness, suggesting that sound, light, and heat are merely perceptions without inherent existence. However, the reception of sound or light by the brain converts them into consciousness—a different form of energy. Even if there were no brain cells to perceive these phenomena, sound and light would still exist as motion rates transmitted through matter or ether, respectively.

Now, all these diverse outcomes represent different rates of motion—the various forms in which energy manifests itself to consciousness, itself a consequence of motion rates transmitted to the brain. Indeed, there seems to be nothing in the universe that does not stem from rates of motion. The mysteries of "occultism" ultimately rest on a physical basis, and it is through physics and physiology that we must seek its elucidation. While we may draw a distinction between the physical and the psychical, it is merely a distinction without a substantive difference.

The esteemed author of the valuable book "Brain and Personality" constructs an intriguing argument to demonstrate that human will is fundamentally distinct from that of lower animals and is, in fact, supernatural. However, an illustration he provides unequivocally proves that will is just as much a form of energy as light, thus precluding any notion of it being supernatural.

He remarks that there is perhaps no term as enshrouded in metaphysical obscurity as the term "Will," and suggests that metaphysicians would do well to eschew metaphysics and focus on physiological facts. While this is commendable advice, I would add that the study of physics should also be incorporated into the proposed course of study.

He proceeds to describe the effect on the visual area of the brain when one eye of an animal is exposed to intense light while the other remains in darkness. The eventual consequence of such overstimulation is a transformation of the normal nerve cell protoplasm, rich in phosphureted fat, into choline and a non-phosphureted neutral fat. He then draws a parallel to the effect on nerve fibers and cells in a specific region of the brain responsible for motor function when continuously stimulated by the will to hold a pen. The resulting condition, akin to writer's palsy, entails degeneration of motive nerve matter and subsequent atrophy of the nerves and muscles they innervate. In both cases, the outcome is an overstimulation-induced alteration, but while the stimulus of light originates externally, that of the will arises internally. Nevertheless, does this internal origin render will any less real than light when it leads to identical physical and chemical changes?

In light of such evidence, it becomes untenable to regard will as anything other than a form of energy. Its locus of force must be sought within, rather than outside, the body—a topic to be explored further in subsequent chapters.

In contemporary discourse, we encounter phrases such as "vital force" and "ever-moving life-force," while thought is increasingly acknowledged as a form of energy. However, feeling has yet to be accorded its rightful place among the various forms of energy.

Life and Death

Confucius, when asked the question, "What is death?" replied, "How can we know what death is, when we do not know what life is?" The great Chinese philosopher was correct. It is only when we understand what life entails that we can truly grasp the concept of death.

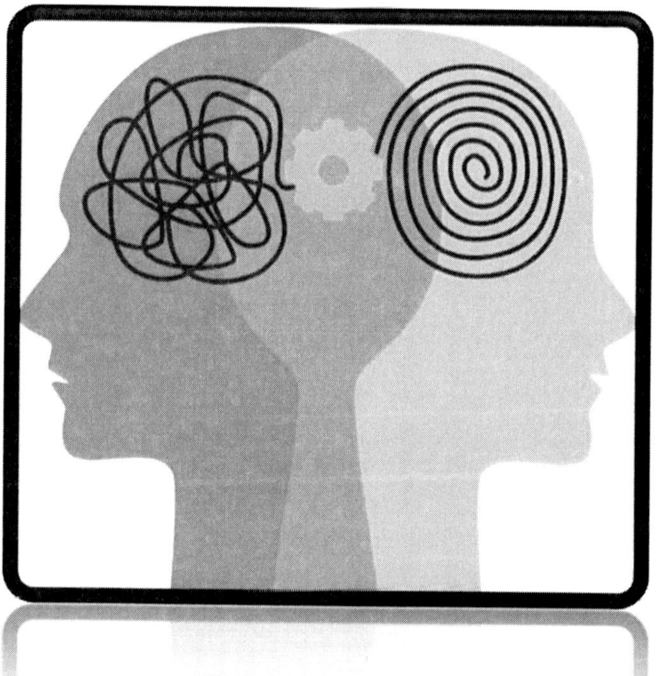

Biologists now use the term "vital force" to describe the power responsible for the sap rising in a tree, while Luther

Burbank speaks of the "ever-moving life-force" that sustains plant and animal life.

There is abundant evidence to suggest that life is a form of energy. For instance, the ability of life, acting through a soft fungus growth in a cellar, to lift heavy slabs of stone flooring should suffice to convince anyone of its considerable force in overcoming resistance. A growing tree can break through seemingly impenetrable substances, and a vine in growth can lift heavy weights. Delicate growing plants can penetrate soil so hard that only significant force could enable them to do so. It has been estimated that this vital force, acting through a sixty-foot elm tree, causes over seven tons of water to evaporate from its seven million leaves into the air within a single summer's day. This quantity is roughly equivalent to the amount of blood that the human heart propels in twenty-four hours.

Now, no one assumes that the heart muscle performs this work independently, just as one would not assume that a pump lifts water without any applied force. The muscle fibers of the heart contract in response to nervous force. This force arises from rates of motion, which can be traced back to vibrations originating in certain nerve cells in the medulla oblongata and are transmitted to the muscular tissue of the heart through nerve fibers known as the intrinsic heart nerves. A second set of nerves regulates the heart's action, while a third set accelerates it. These three sets of nerves, when functioning properly, maintain a balance of power resulting in the heart's normal beating.

However, the body's life does not solely depend on the heart's beating but also on a similar contraction and expansion of the chest and abdominal muscles, facilitating air circulation in the air tubes and cells just as the heart's action facilitates blood circulation in the blood vessels. It is through the coordinated action of these forces sustaining the breathing process and blood circulation that life is sustained in higher animal organisms.

The force required for the human heart to propel nearly eight tons of blood in one day, coursing through arteries, veins, and the intricate network of microscopic capillaries, at such a rapid rate that the entire quantity of blood in the body circulates through the heart in just one to two minutes, with any portion completing a full tour of the body in about twenty-three seconds, is indeed substantial. Likewise, the force exerted by the chest and abdominal muscles, estimated at 500 to 750 pounds, in the act of taking one full breath is no small feat.

Now, these muscles, whose "beating" results in the process of breathing, are also controlled by nerves that carry rates of motion traceable to vibrations within the medulla oblongata, an expansion of the upper part of the spinal cord. "The medulla holds the reins of the pulse and the breath in its hands." There is a small spot in the medulla oblongata that is to the life of the body what the sun is to light—its source, or the vibrating matter that excites the rates of motion, resulting in life. An injury to this spot in the medulla would terminate life as surely as the destruction of the sun would end light, for the same reason—the cessation of vibration of those particles of matter upon which the necessary rates of motion depend for their existence. The heart and muscles of the chest and abdomen "beat" as long as the rates of motion are sustained in the nerves connecting them with the medulla; however, when these rates cease, the beating stops, and death ensues.

It is an interesting question that has not yet been satisfactorily answered: what sustains this action in the medulla? What maintains the vibrations that must never relax or rest from their labor? While other muscles grow tired with continuous action, the involuntary muscles supplied by this force never tire, despite being constantly at work. Physiologists explain this by suggesting that this spot in the medulla is probably a reflex center receiving stimuli from outside, most likely from the blood. Some physiologists consider this action in the medulla to be automatic. The fact that the muscles sustained by this force never tire is attributed by physiologists to the slight rest they receive between each beat.

W. Hanna Thompson considers this explanation inadequate, and I concur with him. He argues that anyone who tries sawing wood, relying on the slight rest their muscles receive between strokes, can soon realize that it is insufficient to prevent exhaustion.

It is evident that the action of particles of matter in the medulla is unique and unlike that which excites rates of motion in the nerves controlling voluntary muscles.

Now, viewing life in the same matter-of-fact, common-sense manner that we regard light or sound, and considering it as matter with which physics is equally concerned, we can find an explanation for this "automatic" action in the medulla of vertebrates, and for a similar action in the "center of force" that sustains the life of any organism.

Lower forms of animal life, as well as plant life, consist of a single cell, meaning they are unicellular. As they grow, they divide and separate, with each cell becoming two. This process is known as propagation by division. Higher forms of animal and plant life are colonies of such cells, known as multicellular organisms. Their life is vastly superior and infinitely more complex, as they possess organs and various types of tissue, each composed of different types of cells.

The theory I propose, which I believe will withstand criticism, is as follows:

The life of a unicellular organism (whether plant or animal) is sustained by the action of two forces, each representing a rate of motion, such that their union produces waves that combine in successive reinforcements and interferences, resulting in a palpitation effect, known as a "beat." This effect occurs when two tuning forks of different vibration rates are set in motion simultaneously, or when a black and an adjacent white key on a piano are struck together. When sound waves unite in like phases, their crests combine, resulting in increased sound volume. When they unite in opposite phases, the crests of one set coincide with the troughs of another, leading to sound cancellation and silence. This phenomenon is called sound interference and is "the leading characteristic property of wave motion."

As mentioned earlier, when two vibration rates combine in a manner that their waves unite in successive reinforcements and interferences, the result is a "beat," and the number of beats per second equals the difference between the two vibration rates. This action will persist as long as the vibrations continue, resulting in life. However, when the vibrations cease, there will be complete interference without corresponding reinforcement, leading to death. It is crucial to remember that this latter action is "the leading characteristic property of wave motion," and life, viewed as a form of energy, must stem from the action of motion rates, which should be regarded exactly as we view wave motion resulting in sound or light. The fact that in all forms of life, whether plant or animal, there are two forces—male and female—represented in each organism, and that there is no absolute male or female existence in all life, one separate from the other, supports the conclusion that life and death are the outcomes of such force actions as described.

In multicellular organisms, whether plant or animal, development originates from a germ cell resulting from the fusion of two unicellular organisms, each representing a different motion rate. In the fusion of two such cells, each representing two motion rates, there should be two sets of waves, uniting in successive reinforcements and interferences, and consequently, two beats. This is precisely what we observe in higher animal organisms—two beats of different rates, with four heartbeats for every cycle of chest and abdominal muscle contractions. In plants, although no noticeable beating is observed, there must be some such action of life forces in some center of force, for they too have their breathing process and circulation. In the human body, this force action is sustained, as previously mentioned, in a small spot in the medulla oblongata.

Recently, a very delicate instrument has been invented to determine the sex of an egg. When held above an egg containing the germ cell that will develop into a male bird, the instrument shows a rotary movement, while above an egg from which a female will develop, it shows a pendulous movement. At first glance, this might seem to contradict the theory previously stated; if the motion rate communicated by the male cell is rotary and that by the female cell is pendulous, they could not unite in the manner in which sound waves unite to produce a "beat." However, the cells contained in the eggs experimented upon are not the unicellular organisms referred to, but the germ cells (multi-cellular) resulting from the fusion of unicellular organisms.

Death is to life what darkness is to light—what silence is to sound. The organism's life depends on the constant renewal of its tissue cells. Millions of blood cells are exhaled with every breath. Life is impossible without its intermediate state, death, which interposes between states of existence as silence between sounds. The sun is not only the great source of light but also of life. The earth moves in the magnetic field of the sun, and all life upon the earth would cease to exist if the sun were blotted out of existence. Death and darkness would reign together.

Death should not evoke horror in the mind. There can be nothing but good in a law that is so essential to the great plan upon which the universe is built.

Consciousness must end with brain activity, as it is directly the result of such activity. However, this does not prove that we do not possess a larger consciousness belonging to a "spiritual body" composed of psychomeres, as some learned men believe, and as "New Light on Immortality," a new work by a French scholar, E. E. Fournier D'Albe, B. Sc., A. R. C. Sc., teaches.

Even if it is proven that when we die, a part of us leaves our body and continues to exist in some form within the Earth's atmosphere, it does not necessarily mean our soul lives forever. It simply suggests that there might be another phase of existence after this one, a continuation of who we are that could last forever, but it does not prove it.

When someone we deeply love dies suddenly, it is incredibly painful. If we did not have the hope of seeing them again in a better place, it would be hard to cope with the grief. Throughout history, people have wished to reunite with those they have lost in a happier afterlife. This strong desire suggests there might be something to it. If indeed there is another life after this one, we can only guess what amazing experiences and reunions it might bring.

However, instead of focusing too much on what might come after, let us focus on making the most of the life we have now. Let us cherish every moment and enjoy every little thing it has to offer.

The Laws of Motion

All the different ways energy manifests follow certain clear and precise rules. For instance, if an object falls freely, the distance it travels in any given number of seconds can be calculated using a specific formula.

Since movement is fundamental in the universe and is essential for life and awareness, it's highly valuable to delve into Newton's laws of motion. These laws aren't limited to celestial bodies like planets; they apply universally, even to minuscule particles invisible to the strongest microscopes. They govern every aspect of waves, including individual components and the waves themselves. Newton's laws even extend to every atom in our bodies and to our bodies as a whole.

Newton's laws of motion also elucidate the vibrations occurring in every nerve and blood cell in our bodies, which are responsible for our thoughts, feelings, and even our will. Therefore, it's crucial to emphasize that studying Newton's laws of motion can significantly enhance our understanding of how things operate and dispel confusion stemming from excessive contemplation of metaphysics.

Now, let's examine Newton's laws:

1. Objects remain at rest or in uniform motion in a straight line unless acted upon by an external force.
2. The acceleration of an object is directly proportional to the net force acting on it and inversely proportional to its mass.
3. For every action, there is an equal and opposite reaction.

For example, when you hold a ball, it stays stationary until you exert force with your muscles to throw it. Upon release, gravity pulls the ball downward to the ground.

In the simple act of throwing a ball, all three of Newton's laws are evident. The ball would have remained stationary if not for your throw. The force exerted by your arm caused the ball to move in the direction of the throw, with the distance traveled dependent on the force applied. Additionally, the ball's reaction exerted an equal force back onto your hand, as per the third law.

It's been suggested that our thoughts and feelings can affect us, influencing our experiences of love or hatred based on our focus. Understanding our bodies and how Newton's laws apply can demystify this phenomenon.

The vibrations in our brains generate waves in the surrounding space, akin to a center of energy. The intensity of our thoughts and feelings dictates the speed and direction of these vibrations. Stronger vibrations produce more significant waves, similar to how wind generates larger waves on water. These waves extend in all directions, forming a sphere around us that permeates through the earth and the air, aided by the earth's transmission properties, akin to electricity.

For these waves to have a substantial impact and travel far, our thoughts, willpower, and emotions must be intense and powerful.

Applying the first law of motion to our nerve centers reveals that they remain inactive or potentially harmful until external stimuli prompt action, whether from external sources or within our bodies.

Certain thoughts may dominate our minds until another force, such as willpower or external stimuli, alters our focus.

Emotions can persist with varying intensity until influenced by thoughts, willpower, or external factors.

Willpower can remain weak or obstinately strong until influenced by thoughts, emotions, or external forces. While weak wills are easily swayed, stubborn ones require a significant force to change.

A strong will isn't inherently stubborn; it can be guided by rational thoughts and emotions. However, altering its course still necessitates a substantial force.

The human will is tremendously potent, and we're only scratching the surface of its full potential.

It's crucial to recognize that we're always enveloped by wave motion. Ether and air waves consistently interact with our bodies. When these waves transmit varying rates of motion to the brain via our nerves, we perceive sensations, which are perceptions of external stimuli. This differs from internal feelings originating from nerve centers within our bodies.

However, not all waves that touch our bodies affect the action of our nerve centers, hence we don't always feel their presence.

For instance, during a wireless telegraphy demonstration by De Forest, waves emitted from the transmitter passed through the bodies of everyone present without their awareness, as noted by Prof. W. J. Clarke in an article published in the Chicago "American."

Just like sound waves emanate from a vibrating body and electricity waves transmit from a wireless transmitter, the waves generated by vibrations in our brain cells also propagate in spherical patterns. These waves operate akin to air waves causing sound and ether waves producing electricity.

Similar to sound, light, and heat waves, these waves stimulate analogous vibrations in a receiving device attuned to pick them up. It's not only logical but also unreasonable to think otherwise. Much like how light, heat, and sound waves reflect, and electricity behaves like an echo, the waves generated by our nerve vibrations interact similarly.

Reflection commonly occurs with light, heat, and sound waves. For instance, a voice sounds different in various rooms due to sound wave reflection. When similar waves reinforce each other, they amplify, making the sound louder. Amplitude, denoting the distance between the highest and lowest points of a wave's motion, determines the sound's volume and force.

All wave motions share identical properties. The waves generated by our nerve vibrations also adhere to the law of action and reaction, sometimes intensifying when synchronized with similar waves.

If we persistently dwell on negative thoughts and feelings, we're likely to attract adversity. This is evidenced by experience and aligns with the law of action and reaction.

Even amidst distressing circumstances, succumbing to chronic despair and self-pity only binds us to unhappiness. To improve our situations, we must shift our mindset towards positivity, as our actions inevitably yield corresponding outcomes.

Life is often likened to a magician's cup overflowing with our contributions, illustrating Newton's third law of motion—the law of action and reaction.

To attain our desired outcomes, our efforts must be resolute and unwavering. We should harbor optimistic and joyful desires, directing our willpower, thoughts, and emotions towards our goals.

Our nerve centers should be stimulated with firm, strong, and definite desires, guided by our brain centers. Maintaining control over our thoughts and feelings is crucial to manifesting positive outcomes, as malevolent thoughts can yield adverse consequences, while benevolent and wholesome thoughts can bring about good.

Understanding that conditions are in constant flux, with forces perpetually acting and reacting, allows us to exert influence and steer events in our favor.

Every action or change in motion corresponds to the applied force and is proportionate to it. However, we often underestimate the power of our bodies. Instead of relying on external factors, we should seize control and realize our inherent potential.

As we take action for ourselves, we swiftly witness our strength growing, persisting, and continuing to evolve. Just as disasters tend to occur in clusters, so do favorable conditions—they gravitate towards the center of force, where positive actions generate waves that attract more positivity.

We're continually enveloped by waves, both negative and positive, akin to heat, light, and sound waves. Happiness flows abundantly and unexpectedly when we induce the right kind of action in our spinal nerve centers.

Hope is a potent force for good, but it must be genuine and spirited. Hope lacking in energy and spirit isn't truly hope; it's merely a hollow imitation.

The Human Body

I find nothing more astonishing than the human body, with its intricate network of nerves and blood vessels, its marvelously designed digestive system, its muscle tissue, and its various organs, each with its specific function, even when facing the challenges of ill health. Each tiny cell acts as an individual, contributing to the delicate balance of health when guided wisely by the nerve centers.

Even the seemingly unsightly skeletal structure is a remarkably clever design, serving not only to convert nervous energy into mechanical energy but also to protect the delicate organs.

Dr. R. Hutchinson praises the human skin, calling it the most incredible fabric in the world. It's flexible like silk, strong like steel, beautifully tinted, tough like leather, and almost see-through. It's an outstanding insulator against electricity, incredibly resilient, and capable of remarkable self-repair. With a network of blood vessels capable of holding half the body's blood, it can adapt to extreme temperatures. With nearly three million sweat glands, it's incredibly efficient at self-cleaning. Very little can penetrate the skin; even most medicines applied topically are either evaporated by body heat and inhaled by the lungs or merely affect the mind through their appearance and scent.

The wonders of the skin are impressive, but they don't compare to the marvels of the nervous system and circulation. Every cell depends on the nervous system for guidance and the circulation for nourishment. and it's the nerves that regulate the heart and blood vessels, controlling our circulation. Even our breathing relies on nerves that manage the respiratory muscles.

The spinal system was the original nervous system, appearing first in embryonic development. In the medulla oblongata, the life forces initiated during cell division in the original germ cell continue their work in the human body.

The nerve centers of the spinal system still direct the movements of every muscle, while the higher nerve centers added through evolution serve as control centers. Each nerve center has its specific role, acting according to a predetermined plan, even though some movements may seem consciously directed due to habitual actions.

The cerebrum, known as the center of thought activity and consciousness, is located in the front and upper part of the skull.

However, the cerebellum, situated at the back of the head below the cerebrum, remains somewhat mysterious.

The cerebellum contains a different arrangement of nerve matter compared to other nerve centers, likely explaining its distinct functions. It appears to control voluntary muscles because when it's removed from animals, they lose control over these muscles. Their movements become uncertain, with less vigor and purpose.

Since willpower controls voluntary muscles, removing the cerebellum essentially removes the organ through which will acts on other nerve centers. This suggests that the cerebellum is the seat of will, just as the cerebrum is the seat of intelligence. It makes sense in an organism designed for the use of soul-powers to have specific centers of action for each.

Will is considered a form of energy, and like all forms of energy, it's the result of certain rates of motion. This motion, which manifests as will, likely originates from the vibrations of nerve particles in the cerebellum. Destroying the cerebellum would therefore eliminate will, much like destroying the sun would eliminate light.

While light travels in waves through ether, will has its own pathways in the nervous system, conveying its motion to other nerve centers. Will must work alongside thought for actions to have purpose. Essentially, the human body functions as a power-house, converting one form of energy into another. Each form of energy has its designated center of action: thought in the cerebrum, will in the cerebellum, life forces in the medulla oblongata, and the spinal reflex centers facilitate the conversion of these forces into mechanical energy by causing muscle contractions and movements.

My intention in discussing the human body isn't to provide detailed descriptions of its organs and functions, as one would find in a physiology textbook. Rather, I aim to draw deductions by comparing facts from physiology and physics.

Another form of energy results from the rates of motion communicated to the cerebrum by blood in the arteries, dependent on the heart's action. These are purely psychical feelings. The intensity of these feelings varies with the strength or weakness of the heart's action. For instance, what might incite anger in one person could leave another unaffected due to differences in heart action.

In cases where the brain is exposed due to injury, emotions like pain, anger, or fear have been observed to cause the brain to protrude and pulsate with arterial pulsations.

Just as asserting the will can be felt in the cerebellum causing muscle tension, strong feelings direct attention to the heart as their center of action. This reaffirms the ancient belief that the heart is the center of feelings and passions.

The reflex centers not only receive stimuli from external forces but also from internal centers of force within the body. Our thoughts, feelings, and will influence these centers, forming habits of thinking, feeling, willing, and muscular action.

The human body is truly deserving of profound admiration. Consider the remarkable human eye, with its expressive powers and intricately constructed parts, each playing a role in receiving and focusing light rays onto the retina. The optic nerve then transmits these impulses to the visual area of the cerebrum.

The wonders of the eye are matched by those of the ear, a remarkable device for receiving, modifying, and transmitting sound. Inside the ear's chamber are delicate fibers arranged in a spiral, resembling a microscopic harp with thousands of strings. If one could strike these chords, they could reproduce every tone distinguishable by the ear.

The remarkable ability of the vocal organs to produce and modify sounds is truly admirable. Through practice and habit, these organs can articulate up to 1,500 letters per minute, each requiring precise positioning. The human voice, with its modulations and capacity for conveying thoughts and emotions through words, tones, and music, is a precious asset. However, we often fail to fully appreciate or utilize it to enhance our own happiness and that of others. It possesses great power for both good and evil.

We often hear about the art of reading character. One significant aspect of character expression is reflected in the tones of the voice. Soft tones are generally pleasing, unless they carry a hint of insincerity or deception. A useful approach to cultivating a desirable oral expression is to cultivate positive thoughts and emotions that we wish to convey. It's the struggle of undesirable thoughts and feelings seeking expression that makes the voice unpleasant. A soft voice that seems insincere can be as unpleasant as harsh and grating tones to those who can detect the lack of genuineness.

The human body serves as the vessel through which souls can connect with one another. Even if it's considered just the outer covering of the spiritual body we're said to have, it's still remarkable. We should be grateful for the opportunity to inhabit it and strive to honor and cherish it rather than discard it.

The Great Law of Habit

We often casually mention that we're creatures of habit, but we don't fully grasp the significance of this truth. Habit is a profound law, one of the fundamental laws of life. Understanding how habits form is crucial because we're constantly developing habits, whether they're beneficial or harmful. A habit becomes a dominating force that controls us, often without us realizing it until we attempt to break free from its hold. If we take a moment to assess our habits, we'll be surprised by their abundance and diversity.

Habit plays a significant role in our lives. It's what makes our bodies function smoothly and accomplish amazing things. Let me break it down for you: First, our nerves detect what's happening around us. Then, they send that information to our brain. The brain then instructs our muscles on what actions to take, and they respond accordingly. When we repeat the same actions over and over, like a daily routine, it becomes a habit. Initially, our brain guides our muscles, but eventually, they perform these actions automatically, without us even thinking about it. Our spine, part of our backbone, helps in this process by taking some of the load off our brain, ensuring things run smoothly. Once a habit forms, our spine prefers to stick to it, even if our brain wants to change it. Our muscles quickly adapt to follow the spine's lead, becoming more skilled at performing familiar tasks. It's essential to recognize the spine's crucial role and how it influences our behavior.

All our strength lies in the spinal nerve-centers. They are unreasoning dolts, but they perform, unerringly, that which the brain centers train them to do, and have no choice but to do as they are bidden, and constantly grow in power. Without them the brain is powerless to move a muscle; it is as helpless without their support and co-operation as a king deserted by army, navy and parliament. It is that mechanical action of these nerve-centers of the spinal cord, which we call Habit—the tendency to repeat an action, whether mental or physical, which the brain centers begin.

The person who started drinking didn't think they'd end up addicted. They didn't imagine that drinking would become the most important thing in their life, leading them to a low point. Even now, in their miserable state, they don't really know what caused their downfall. It's not just the alcohol that ruined them; it's the habit. They don't understand how their body works, or that they've trained their spinal nerve centers to react a certain way to certain triggers. These nerve centers keep responding the same way until they're trained otherwise. The person may blame alcohol, but until they deal with the real issue — their habit — their nerves will keep reacting the same way whenever they encounter anything related to drinking. It's these triggers that keep us stuck in our habits. The nerve centers take cues from the signals sent to them through our senses, following the instructions from our brain. Unless we send stronger signals to change these habits, they'll keep doing what they've been doing.

In creatures without advanced brains, like some vertebrates, the spinal nerve centers just react automatically to outside forces, following a fixed pattern due to habit. With higher brain centers, there's some control over this. Our voluntary actions can be guided by these higher centers.

We've been taught that every action leaves a mark in our nerve centers, making us more likely to do it again. But we might not realize how crucial this is. Habit — this tendency for nerve centers to repeat actions — is what enables us to do basic things like walking and talking, as well as more complex tasks. Without habit, we'd be unable to learn or do anything meaningful.

Musicians, for instance, become skilled through habit. It's how we learn anything. So, it's important to understand the power of habit. It's a force that takes over anything we start and continues it without us even thinking about it, gaining strength as we feed it until it controls us completely. This power isn't just relevant to addicts; it affects us all. Before we judge those struggling with addiction, we should consider how much we ourselves are controlled by habit. Many of our failures and problems can be traced back to this force if we bother to look.

It's thanks to habit that the saying "Practice makes perfect" holds true. We can't achieve any level of skill without it. The spinal nerve centers quickly learn to make our muscles move in response to certain triggers, without needing input from the brain centers. A musician who once had to concentrate on every note and finger movement can eventually play complex pieces effortlessly. Initially clumsy when the brain had to guide every action, once the spinal centers take over, skill emerges. What was once awkward becomes charming, soothing even.

This process isn't limited to music or other talents. It applies to everything we do. Our nerve centers have a strong tendency to repeat actions, shaping our lives significantly. While we're aware of how easily habits form, we often overlook that most of our actions, especially the skilled ones, are habitual. Once actions become habits, we must ensure they're not harmful. Overeating or extreme greed can become habits to the point of self-destruction. We might call it "mania," but it's just another form of habit. Habit is powerful and often looks to the brain centers for guidance, which can be flawed and weak, lacking an understanding of their own power and the influence they should have over the nerve centers.

Whether we're ill-natured or good-natured isn't so much about circumstances or temperament as it is about habit. Anyone can develop the habits they desire if their determination is strong enough. The higher nerve centers have the job of controlling the lower ones, which act according to orders with great efficiency. They never say "I can't" when given orders, as long as their cells are healthy and the nerves can carry messages to the muscles. They immediately start working to carry out the required movements with unwavering obedience, much like soldiers following orders without question. It's important, then, to be mindful of what commands we give these loyal soldiers. The reasoning and decision-making should come from the higher authority of the nerve centers. An army with a weak and incapable commander poses a threat to the safety of a nation.

The claims being made about our incredible abilities might seem exaggerated and silly to some, but they're backed by physiological facts. Physiologists, who are not known for exaggeration, explain that desire activates the brain's motor centers, which then signal the spinal centers to stimulate muscle contractions, leading to specific movements needed to fulfill that desire. This process isn't straightforward and can involve consciousness and even a delay between the desire and the action, as seen in someone longing to visit Europe, whose desire might only materialize after many years.

This statement, taken from Martin's "Human Body," used in public schools, deserves serious consideration. It reveals a lot about the role of habit in our subconscious actions, a topic much discussed nowadays. The way the spinal centers obediently respond to desire is remarkable. Desire acts as a stimulus on these nerve centers, just like light or electricity, compelling them to respond accordingly. Even though the response to desire may not be as immediate as pulling away from a hot stove, if the desire is strong and persistent, the nerve centers will continue to work until the desired outcome is achieved. When desire becomes a habit, it becomes a powerful force that guides the nerve centers to formulate plans and execute them until the desire is fulfilled.

Unexpected help or opportunities, seemingly random, are actually governed by certain laws of physics discussed earlier. If desire is inconsistent or weak, it won't sustain the nerve centers' efforts, leading to uncertain results. However, if desire is strong and unwavering, results will come much sooner, even if the effort is consistent but lacks intensity.

It's habit that drives our actions and thoughts, whether it's habitual thinking or behavior. We become more capable of acting and thinking by repeating those actions and thoughts until they become habits.

Those trapped by undesirable habits often lament, "If only I hadn't started." It's right at the beginning that habit slowly but surely ensnares us. It's like the spider enticing the unsuspecting fly into its web with promises of delights. Once we've foolishly entangled ourselves, habit mockingly asks, "Will you leave now?"

Due to our ignorance of how our nerve centers work and our disregard for their tendency to repeat actions, we allow habit to grow stronger until we become its obedient servants. The addict will sacrifice anything for their fix, whether it's the opium fiend selling their soul or the drunkard taking food from their children for alcohol. We truly are creatures of habit.

From the moment we're born, habit starts managing our actions, thoughts, and feelings. Our brain centers set things in motion, and it's their job to keep them going. This is how we gain physical and intellectual strength. Neglecting one over the other is not beneficial, as the body and mind should always maintain a balance of power.

Habits of Self-Control

Self-control means the brain centers properly managing the spinal nerve centers to allow only desirable habits to form. While we often hear of people praised for having "perfect self-control," it's crucial to understand that the brain centers must remain vigilant to keep these habit-forming centers in check. This highlights the truth of the saying "Eternal vigilance is the price of power," especially in how the brain interacts with the spinal nervous system.

The spinal system constantly seeks autonomy from the brain, forming habits without our awareness of the power we've given to these nerve centers. Small actions like fidgeting with hair or clothing, wrinkling the forehead, or biting nails are easily picked up by the spinal system and repeated unconsciously. We may not even realize these actions have become habits, emphasizing how active and in need of guidance the spinal nervous system truly is.

"Nervousness" stems from a lack of self-control or assertiveness by the brain centers in managing the spinal centers. However, by maintaining calmness and directing attention to the spinal nervous system while firmly asserting the desire for calmness, we can quiet the nerves and regain self-control. Adopting a posture of closing the hands firmly against the palms surprisingly stimulates the spinal system when conveying the commands we want it to follow.

A self-possessed individual doesn't let their spinal nerves engage in useless actions. Using W. Hanna Thompson's analogy of the brain centers as the rider and the spinal system as the horse, the self-controlled person is like the skilled horseman. In moments requiring self-control, their brain centers guide the "horse" to navigate obstacles smoothly, while a nervous rider might panic and make mistakes. Given the spinal system's tendency to take control, it's essential to guide it firmly.

Habits play a significant role in our lives, shaping our actions and behaviors. However, we have the power to choose what habits we develop. We can form habits of overworking or idleness, of constantly being busy or withdrawing from society, of worrying excessively or lazily drifting through life, of being argumentative or lacking motivation. The tendency of habit-forming nerve centers is to push us to extremes in whatever behaviors we allow them to engage in. We often find ourselves caught up in actions we don't want to do and know are not beneficial, feeling as though we can't control it. But the truth is, we can.

Our spinal system, likened to a horse, will continue in one direction until we redirect it onto a different path. It's always restless, needing to be occupied, even if it's just with thoughts. If we don't guide it firmly, we lose control and our self-possession suffers.

Idle thinking lacks strength and easily shifts from one conclusion to another. When we bounce between different courses of action without certainty, we don't gain power or stability. True strength and resourcefulness come from knowing, not just thinking. We must strive to know what is right and follow that path consistently.

We must reflect seriously on the habits that govern our lives. Are we using our brain centers to properly control the spinal system, or are we allowing them to lead us into aimless or harmful activities? If we don't guide them correctly, they'll carry out those actions, leading to fruitless busyness and unsatisfactory outcomes.

If we allow our thoughts to wander aimlessly, our hands and feet to engage in pointless movements, and our lips to speak without thought, this soon becomes a habit, resulting in nothing but wasted energy. Gaining self-control requires effort. As someone wisely remarked, "Don't start your mouth going and then leave it." We can only eliminate undesirable habits by cultivating desirable ones because we must form habits to be active. Without forming habits, we cannot function. All our actions and thoughts are mere mistakes until they become habitual. If it weren't for the law of habit, we would still be learning to walk, always attempting but never truly learning anything.

However, we must remember that the spinal nerve centers cannot differentiate between good and bad habits. We can learn harmful behaviors just as easily as desirable ones and become as skilled in them. Therefore, we must control not only our actions but also our thoughts and feelings because they too become habitual and can spiral out of control if left unchecked.

The will is a dominant force within us, often asserting itself with the stubbornness of a tyrant, insisting on its desires even when reason suggests otherwise. The spinal system must obey this will and carry out its commands, as the saying goes, "Where there's a will, there's a way." However, this isn't true self-control. The will must be guided by both knowledge and emotion. These three forces must work together harmoniously for effective self-government and self-control. Ultimately, our power lies in the direction of habit.

If we want to develop self-control, one of the best ways is to start by overcoming undesirable habits and replacing them with positive ones. Dr. Leon Elbert Landone used a method similar to how Luther Burbank trains plants, by breaking bad habits and encouraging the formation of opposite, constructive habits in children. It's impossible for nerve centers to maintain both constructive and destructive habits simultaneously. If children are guided into forming constructive habits, destructive habits will naturally fade away. Just as the tendency to repeat actions applies to all cases involving spinal nerve centers, childhood is a particularly opportune time for habit formation, with bad habits more easily replaced by good ones than in later life. While it's said that "It's hard to teach an old dog new tricks," a person is never too old to change their habits if they have the willpower.

One major reason many people remain trapped in unhappy circumstances is their reluctance to break free from entrenched habits. The tendency is to choose what seems easiest in the moment, often allowing external conditions to control our nerve centers, even when they're undesirable.

The body both generates and transmits energy. We are both creators and products of energy, with our brain centers developing at birth to become generators of energy transmitted to the spinal centers. Yet, it's often easier to let these nerve centers follow their own inclinations than to make them conform to reason, resulting in a haphazard lifestyle.

Habit is the force that drives outcomes, whether good or bad. We have the power to direct it toward creating the conditions we desire. We can't control external circumstances until we control ourselves. If we cultivate habits of self-pity and consistently view ourselves as victims of misfortune, others are more likely to distance themselves from us, reinforcing our sense of isolation. As long as we maintain this mindset and way of speaking, things will inevitably go awry.

The brain centers of a self-controlled individual exert their strongest influence on the spinal centers, preventing them from reacting to stimuli that would provoke undesirable actions like angry outbursts, complaints, or insincere smiles.

Someone with self-control consistently does and says the appropriate things at the right moments. Poise, synonymous with self-control, represents a balanced state of power. It involves the nerve centers functioning in an orderly manner, with the higher centers wisely and firmly governing the lower ones, ensuring effective outcomes.

Since we are constantly engaging Habit, it's crucial to determine its focus. One of the most beneficial habits is maintaining a peaceful state of mind—a harmony within the nerve centers, with attention habitually directed towards positive conditions.

A nervous individual struggles to find rest while working, often wasting energy in unnecessary activities until exhaustion forces them to stop. Much of our daily tasks are performed automatically, driven by Habit. During these times, the mind should dwell on peaceful thoughts rather than dwelling on troubles or fretting over obstacles.

When the mind is trained to adopt restful attitudes and focus on positive aspects, work becomes much easier and less fatiguing compared to worrying about tasks or other matters. Constant inner turmoil breeds trouble, leading to sickness, discord, and failure. Maintaining inner calmness helps preserve the balance crucial for health, happiness, and success.

Habit and Disease

Our understanding of Habit should have long ago suggested to us that many disease symptoms are actually habits. If you examine the symptoms of almost any illness, you're likely to find at least one that can be identified as a habit, often responsible for the other symptoms.

In ancient times, people believed that diseases were caused by evil spirits, which was closer to the truth than the modern belief attributing everything to microbes and resorting to toxins to eliminate them. In reality, it's not evil spirits that control us during sickness, but Habit taking charge and dictating our condition. Instead of blindly combating diseases with knives and poisons, we need to look beyond microbes to identify the true cause of illness. Microbes are just one aspect of diseased conditions, not the root cause of the disease itself.

We should focus on addressing the source of disease and crime rather than just dealing with the symptoms. Only by eliminating the root cause can we stop the effects. For too long, we've been preoccupied with managing criminals and treating the sick without addressing the underlying causes of crime and disease. As long as these causes remain unchecked, crime and illness will continue to thrive, and institutions like hospitals, prisons, surgeons, and executioners will have no shortage of victims.

One significant contributor to the rise in degeneracy and criminal behavior is the widespread use of intoxicants and drugs among mothers in urban areas. This harmful habit, along with the stressful and nerve-wracking urban lifestyle, serves as a breeding ground for crime and disease. Such habits are often adopted to cope with difficult circumstances, which are sometimes imposed by societal norms.

However, it's not just cities where these problems arise. Even in rural areas, where life is considered more honest and wholesome, serious crimes occur. It's not the location but rather Habit that plays a significant role in the prevalence of crime and disease. Until individuals grasp the power of Habit and educate their children to control it rather than being controlled by it, we cannot expect a reduction in crime and illness.

The only way to control the power of Habit is by redirecting it—giving it something positive to focus on. While we've understood in a general sense what Habit can do for us, we haven't fully appreciated its magnitude. We might not be able to stop Habit's influence entirely, but we can prevent it from harming us by harnessing its energy for our benefit. Habit is a force that can either uplift us or lead to our downfall, and it tirelessly works on whatever task we assign to it.

We're familiar with how Habit shapes the skills of a talented pianist, but we often overlook the fact that we can become just as proficient in habits like coughing, spitting, or blowing our noses as we can in more conventional skills like skating or playing the piano. Whatever we repeatedly practice, Habit ensures that we become increasingly skilled at it, including behaviors we associate with disease symptoms. When we engage in habits, whether in thought or action, that harm our body tissues, we pave the way for potential health issues. Microbes may exacerbate these conditions, but they are a secondary factor in the development of disease—they are an effect rather than a cause.

Symptoms like those of catarrh are essentially habits that can be broken just like any other habit—by forming new habits and consciously avoiding anything associated with the condition. By steering clear of stimuli like handkerchiefs or places where symptoms typically arise, we can disrupt the habitual responses of our spinal nerve-centers. These nerve-centers are predisposed to trigger specific movements based on the stimuli they've been trained to respond to, much like how a drunkard is compelled to reach for another drink.

We shouldn't attempt to fight habits; instead, we must replace them by cultivating new habits, starting with habits of thought. To overcome disease, we must fill our minds with thoughts of happiness and envision the best possible conditions we desire to experience. Our hearts should be filled with the belief that everything is as we wish it to be.

Rather than acknowledging and focusing on the presence of disease, we should speak and think about health. This mindset will activate our nerve-centers to work towards creating healthy conditions within us. When we constantly remind ourselves of the presence of disease and maintain habits that reinforce its symptoms, our nerve-centers receive stimuli from both external sources and our own thought processes. Under such circumstances, disease becomes inevitable, with stronger internal stimuli from our thoughts leading to more severe manifestations of illness.

However, if we change the type of stimuli we send to our nerve-centers, instructing them to disregard external triggers and focus on promoting health, Habit will work to rebuild what it previously tore down. Dr. Landone suggests that almost any tissue can be regenerated through wise and conservative approaches.

In "Brain and Personality," W. Hanna Thompson discusses asthma, highlighting how habits formed during childhood, such as coughing extensively during whooping cough, can lead to long-lasting breathing patterns that contribute to asthma. This underscores the importance of being mindful of the habits we cultivate, especially during formative stages of life.

"When the normal breathing habits become disrupted, the respiratory center may become sensitive to various afferent stimuli that would normally go unnoticed in a healthy state. For example, one type of asthma, known as 'cat asthma,' can be triggered by the mere presence of a cat in the room, even if the patient is unaware of the animal's presence." Another example involves buckwheat flour having a similar effect. These peculiar reactions of the condition highlight the risk of disturbing old, normal nervous habits.

It's evident that these triggering objects, such as a cat or buckwheat flour, were somehow associated with the habit when it initially formed. The responsibility falls on the asthmatic individual to break the unhealthy breathing habit by cultivating deep and regular breathing patterns during times when external stimuli are not influencing them. They should also consider these external stimuli, to which their nerve-centers have been accustomed, as inferior to the guidance provided by the higher brain-centers within.

As long as the higher brain-centers allow external stimuli to dictate the responses of the spinal centers, undesirable habits will continue to control the body. These higher centers must exert their influence to restrain the spinal centers and encourage the formation of more beneficial habits.

The healing attributed to "change of climate" is actually the result of a shift in habits, brought about by removing oneself from the objects and conditions that trigger the stimuli keeping the nerve-centers engaged in maintaining disease symptoms. When a person, essentially enslaved by habit, relocates to a new environment, they forget about the thoughts and objects that kept them bound to illness, allowing their nervous system to engage in more beneficial activities. However, in cases where changing climate doesn't lead to a cure, it's because the individual fails to mentally detach from their old conditions, thus preventing the stimuli from new surroundings to influence their habits. Habits of thought precede habits of action, and until the individual's focus shifts towards new and positive conditions, they remain bound by the old ones.

The power to heal lies within the brain-centers. They possess the ability and responsibility to control the habit-forming centers, as bestowed by nature. Through the "private wires" connecting them, the brain-centers can exert stronger stimuli on the spinal centers than external objects, provided they are activated or prompted to utilize their inherent power.

The problem arises from our historical fear and superstition regarding disease, leading us to neglect understanding the mechanics of our bodies and feeling powerless in the face of what seemed like an inexplicable mystery. However, if we experience any disease symptoms, it's essential to determine whether they stem from habits. Once we ascertain that they do, we have the means of cure readily available within the higher nerve-centers of our bodies. Habits of thought, more than anything else, bind the spinal system to diseased conditions, while afferent stimuli from the surrounding environment provide the impulses necessary to sustain these symptoms.

Any object associated with the habit of frequent spitting, a common symptom of catarrh, will trigger throat accumulation as reliably as the presence of a cat will induce wheezing in a person with "cat asthma." If a spittoon has been linked to the habit of spitting, it will attract someone suffering from catarrh like a magnet.

The timing of certain activities, such as going to bed at night or waking up in the morning, can exacerbate catarrh if it has been troublesome during those times, as they provide the customary stimuli to which the nerve-centers have become accustomed to responding. Certain times of the year or atmospheric conditions can also revive old habits associated with disease symptoms.

Factors like time, location, objects, thoughts, willpower, and emotions all contribute to the formation of habits that manifest as disease symptoms.

The solution lies in redirecting habits to a more beneficial use. Willpower, thoughts, and emotions should inhibit the habit-forming nerve-centers, and if new environments, objects, and conditions can replace the old ones, the task becomes easier, as there are no former influences obstructing the response to stimuli. When a patient is cured and reintroduced to the old influences that contributed to the formation of disease symptoms, it's not uncommon for those symptoms to resurface. If the patient comprehends the influence of these old associations on their nerve-centers, they can, with sufficient willpower, control their spinal system through thought and emotion, thereby breaking the habit of responding to external influences. Internal stimuli supersede external stimuli in efficacy, and it is upon this realization that we must rely for cures, rather than resorting to the harmful habit of ingesting drugs to alleviate symptoms.

Habits of Thought

"Sow a thought and reap an act; sow an act and reap a habit." When experiencing great distress of mind, people sometimes express, "If I could only stop thinking! It is this thinking that is driving me to distraction." The only way to cease dwelling on distressing thoughts is to redirect our focus onto something else. Our thoughts and feelings can be controlled if our desire to do so is strong enough. However, if we allow habit to maintain a certain pattern of thinking in the brain centers, which we have trained it to sustain, it will continue to exert its powerful influence over us, making us feel as though we cannot escape being governed by distressing thoughts. This pattern of thinking is akin to any other habit and can be broken in the same manner—by consciously cultivating habits of an opposite nature.

Many people maintain a wretched mental attitude out of a sense of duty. If misfortune befalls us, it has become customary to mourn for so long that it has evolved into a kind of religious practice. For some, it is still considered a sign of noble character to dwell on every possible aspect of misery and to present it at every opportunity. However, this philosophy is gradually fading away, and the growing prevalence of cultivating positive thought habits, which contribute to creating happier conditions, holds great promise for the future. Our habits of thought consistently influence our lives, whether for good or for ill. Therefore, we must recognize the power of habitual thought and be mindful of how habits shape not only our actions but also our mental well-being.

As an example, there was a woman who, despite her old age, possessed everything necessary to lead a pleasant and fulfilling life. She had wealth and the potential for friendships that could have brought love into her life if she had made herself lovable. However, she closed herself off from others, viewed those around her with suspicion and distrust, withheld love from any living being, and allowed negative thought patterns to dominate her mind. She surrendered herself to the influence of "ugly spells" and allowed these habits of thought to gradually gain control over her until they consumed her completely, leading her to madness. Her episodes of negativity evolved into periodic bouts of maniacal raving. This, without a doubt, was the work of Habit. She was unaware of the immense power that she allowed to govern her, or the extent to which it could drive her.

In the case of any individual suffering from insanity, when it is not the result of physical brain damage, the root cause can often be traced back to habits of thought. The individual has allowed their mind to dwell incessantly on a particular thought or set of thoughts, until habit prevents them from thinking of anything else. Delusions become their reality, with one idea overshadowing all others.

If we find ourselves in an unhappy and seemingly hopeless situation, lamenting that all we can do is think, and viewing thinking as either inconsequential or a source of mental anguish, we are making a grave error. Our ability to think and feel grants us a profound power to lift ourselves out of distress and into the happiness we desire. If we allow our thoughts and emotions to dwell on misery and despair, we are instructing Habit to bind us to such conditions, and Habit unfailingly carries out the directives it is given. If we seek happiness, we must nurture thought habits that align with joyful conditions. We deceive ourselves if we believe, even for a moment, that we can cling to old habits of despondency and misery while expecting positive outcomes. The more we dwell on the belief that everything is working against us, the more vigorously the unconscious forces we are guiding will work to manifest that reality. We must alter our mindset and emotional state if we wish to transcend our unhappy circumstances. Before we can change external circumstances, we must first transform our internal state, and the external world will naturally adjust to reflect this inner change.

We cannot expect to bring about significant changes immediately, just as a skilled pianist cannot instantly master difficult music. However, we can begin to initiate changes and witness results, much like the progress seen in learning to play the piano. As we grow in proficiency and observe encouraging outcomes, we are motivated to persist. If our desire lacks the necessary strength to maintain the nerve-centers' focus on practicing the specific movements essential for achieving our goals, they will divert their attention to forming other habits in response to stronger stimuli.

We can commence making alterations in our circumstances immediately. Even if they are minor, a beginning can always be made, and with sufficient determination, we can progress and enhance our abilities through practice, akin to the pianist. The action of the nerve-centers remains consistent in both scenarios, and the principles that apply to acquiring skill as a pianist also apply to us in pursuing our aspirations.

Succumbing to prevailing conditions and influences spells defeat. However, when we begin by conquering minor difficulties or altering habitual thought patterns, we initiate a process of empowerment that enables us to continue growing in strength. Once we cultivate a habit of overcoming obstacles, we unleash a force capable of lifting us from any situation to another.

The Bible instructs us: "What things soever ye desire when ye pray, believe that ye receive them and ye shall have them," and it further emphasizes that "Faith without works is dead." These teachings, as previously explained, are grounded in principles of physics and physiology.

If we seek happiness, we must embrace the certainty that happiness is within our grasp. It is the immersion in misery and anguish of spirit that triggers the patterns of motion which surround us with unhappy conditions. If this becomes a habit, no other outcome seems possible. Even if external circumstances alter, and we briefly believe we've found happiness, the ingrained habit of unhappiness lingers like a relentless pursuer. We can only shake it off by immersing ourselves in joy, health, and the assurance of success until we develop a habit of believing that everything is conspiring for our good.

As mentioned earlier, we can always initiate changes in our environment. The crucial aspect is taking that initial step. There's always some small action we can undertake, and as we contemplate improving our situation, we discover resources at our disposal that we would have overlooked otherwise. Perhaps it involves rearranging our surroundings or discarding certain sentimental items that unwittingly reinforce old patterns of thought. Clinging to symbols of past sorrow out of a misguided sense of duty is folly. Happiness is not just our right and privilege but also our responsibility.

Objects associated with suffering can indeed draw us into experiencing that suffering. I can grasp the significance of items like the rosary and how they can influence individuals who have long been connected with them, anchoring them to habits of uplifting thought. Any object that anchors us to habits of positive and noble thought is valuable, while those that evoke undesirable habits of thought should be avoided as they pose a real threat. These objects, linked to habits of any kind, whether of thought or action, act as stimuli for the nerve-centers, prompting them to perpetuate such habits. They send signals through the sensory nerves to the nerve-centers, much like sound waves striking the ear and stimulating the auditory nerve, leading to our awareness of what we perceive as sound.

Hereditary tendencies are the outcomes imprinted on the organism by habits passed down through generations. These tendencies could manifest as a predisposition to certain diseases, patterns of intoxication, or even behaviors like kleptomania. However, these tendencies can always be overcome like any habit if they are acknowledged for what they truly are.

Therefore, all this alarming prevalence of crime and disease stems from our familiar companion, Habit, who merely awaits the right direction to labor as diligently and faithfully for health, happiness, and prosperity.

Attention and Habit

Attention serves as the switch by which we direct Habit along any desired path. When we focus our attention on an object or goal, Habit works tirelessly to achieve that objective or advance that purpose. Whatever condition captures our attention, Habit will labor to manifest it.

Therefore, it is crucial how we manage this switch. We can either misuse this powerful tool, allowing it to dissipate its energy on trivial matters, or we can set it on a course that leads us towards the realization of our dreams. Alternatively, choosing the wrong track can result in disaster.

We should learn how to concentrate our attention on what is most desirable. While the value of concentration is widely recognized, its underlying principle is often overlooked. It has been understood for a long time that to learn anything, we must devote our attention to the subject at hand. Attention allows us to acquire knowledge and master skills. This is because Habit takes over once we initiate a process, assuming control and freeing the brain from the burden of attending to details. This enables the brain to direct Habit's power more effectively, which is more than capable of meeting any demands placed upon it. It has long been recognized that proficiency in any endeavor is achieved through this process alone, yet the profound significance of this truth has often eluded us.

Humanity is deeply entrenched in the grip of Habit, to the extent that crime and disease are alarmingly widespread. This should come as no surprise when we consider the degree to which attention is focused on crime and disease. It is well understood that in the process of learning anything, we must devote our attention to it until our actions and thoughts become automatic—controlled by habit—leading us to proficiency. When we direct our attention towards thoughts of disease or crime, we are effectively learning to manifest those conditions. If these thoughts and feelings become habitual, the spinal system will inevitably bring about the realization of the state or condition upon which our attention is fixed. It will lead us to exhibit symptoms of disease until those symptoms solidify into habits. Similarly, attention directed towards crime will lead to criminal behavior, following the same natural process by which attention focused on music leads to musical ability—by prompting actions that develop it. We often say that some people cannot learn music, but this is because they lack sufficient interest to give it their attention.

Habit first operates in the realm of imagination, manifesting in reality what it initially conjures up in the mind. It is through Habit that we possess the power of imagination. In this way, we can accumulate knowledge through memory and the association of ideas and facts presented to our consciousness. We conceive an idea, focus our attention on it, imagine the results, and the same power that initially acts in imagination guides us to formulate plans and find ways to execute them. Great musicians, inventors, artists, and criminals achieve "greatness" in their respective fields because their entire attention is fixed on what interests them most, and Habit takes care of the rest.

If attention is allowed to wander, progress in any endeavor becomes impossible. Conversely, we can always make progress in anything by maintaining our attention on it. The more intense and persistent our concentration, the greater the results.

We should cultivate a habit of thinking and feeling that all things are working together to bring about the conditions we desire—conditions of health, happiness, and success. By doing everything within our power in the present moment, we attract more power to take each subsequent step as needed. Thus, "the future will be the best possible, if we make the present the best possible."

Imagination is a faculty that warrants cultivation. It serves as the designer, while Habit acts as the builder. Effective construction cannot occur without careful design. Since Habit always constructs according to the designs of the imagination, it is crucial that these designs align with what we wish to see become reality. If attention is wavering and uncertain, imagination can engage in little effective design, and the power of habit is diverted.

Both words and objects play significant roles in capturing attention. Words like "Hark! Look! Listen! Remember!" all direct attention and engage all our faculties in a listening stance.

Much has been discussed lately about "going into the silence." This simply entails placing the mind in a state of profound attention; becoming completely still and listening, not to external sounds, but to the silent and potent forces at work within us. In this silent communion with the great forces that constitute our strength, we find a renewal of energy—a restoration of balance.

If we sense that our nerves are unsettled, we should not overlook the opportunity to restore balance in the nerve centers through focusing attention on restful conditions. This calmness is a more potent prayer than any noisy verbal expression that fails to evoke deep emotions.

When our attention is consumed by worry and anxiety disrupts the equilibrium within the nerve centers, we lead a miserable existence and bind ourselves to miserable conditions. We squander our energy in futile fretting because it has become a habit more than a necessity. When we can disregard trivial annoyances and direct our attention toward a noble and worthy purpose, we have taken the right step, and by doing everything within our means at the present moment, we progress (through the law of habit) in knowledge and power.

We have hesitated to focus our attention on our highest and noblest desires, influenced by sayings like, "Don't expect too much, or you will be disappointed," and in the usual way of expecting, this holds true. "We get what we desire, and in just the measure of that desire." If we expect with half-heartedness or in sporadic bursts of overwrought emotions, we fail to control the spinal nerve-centers in a manner that would enable them to work steadily and effectively towards realizing our desires. A resolute and unwavering determination, undeterred by setbacks, will keep the nerve-centers committed to formulating and executing plans until we achieve our desired outcome.

Trivial concerns and irritations lose their ability to distress us when we concentrate on the best and happiest conditions our minds can envision. We have been reluctant to set our minds on lofty ideals, but once we realize that the fulfillment of our desires has a physiological foundation, and that desire functions as a nerve stimulus just like light, compelling the nerve-centers to plan and execute until the desire is fulfilled, we need not hesitate to aim as high as our desires lead us.

When we direct our attention towards the finest and most joyful conditions that our minds can conceive, smaller accomplishments naturally follow suit and seem to come to us effortlessly as we cultivate the habit of expecting the best instead of the worst.

We should avoid the mistake of speaking or thinking about disease. To be well and strong, we must allow healthy conditions to occupy our attention. Some individuals have developed a harmful habit of recounting the symptoms of illnesses. This should not be tolerated. Attention is too valuable a gift to be debased in such a manner. Instead, we should forget undesirable conditions and focus our attention on realizing our deepest aspirations.

☯☯☯

Suggestion and Habi

Despite the growing recognition of the power of suggestion, with auto-suggestion and hypnotic suggestion being increasingly utilized in healing and reforming, dangerous suggestions still abound. Crimes are sensationalized in headlines, and advertisements hinting at diseases are prominently featured in newspapers.

These suggestions serve to draw attention to disease and crime, contributing to the education of individuals in these undesirable paths. For instance, a newspaper article may casually mention that many women commit suicide by jumping off bridges, thereby planting the idea in the minds of those already weakened by misery and despair. Without the redirection of attention through other, stronger suggestions, the spinal nerve-centers will compel the muscles to act upon these suggestions.

The formation of suicide clubs can also be attributed to such suggestions. If every individual, from children to adults, could understand the peril of harboring harmful suggestions and the influence they exert on the nerve-centers responsible for executing actions, crime and disease would encounter formidable resistance from the superior power of the brain-centers. These brain-centers have the ability to redirect attention away from any suggestion that threatens our peace and happiness, providing the spinal system with suggestions of health, happiness, and success to diligently pursue.

When people are aware of the danger posed by harmful suggestions and recognize their own power, such suggestions will find no fertile ground for development. Currently, however, the majority of minds offer favorable conditions for the proliferation of these harmful suggestions.

In order to strengthen the body's defenses against disease, it's crucial to focus attention on healthy and joyful conditions, and fill the mind and heart with uplifting thoughts and feelings. When the mind is happily engaged and the muscles are employed in healthy activities, maintaining a balanced nerve-power, there will be no space for disease to take hold.

It's distressing to consider the fertile ground on which harmful suggestions are being spread—bodies weakened by inadequate nutrition, habitual strain on the nerves due to the rush and stress of modern life, the pressure to maintain appearances and keep up with societal expectations at any cost to health and peace of mind. Already enslaved by Habit, and lacking the knowledge to harness it to their advantage, "the masses" are vulnerable to suggestions of disease and crime. Habits of overtaxing the nerves often lead to drug and alcohol dependencies as a means of seeking temporary relief, despite the fact that this further damages and enslaves the body—a dreadful mistake that could be avoided if the power of suggestion and its relationship to Habit were better understood.

Scolding, fretting, and worrying quickly become habits, keeping the nerve-centers occupied with carrying out these suggestions that stir up trouble.

The only natural way to relieve overworked nerves is through rest. Many perceive rest as purely physical, and while they may place their bodies in a restful position, they allow their minds to continue worrying about cares and problems. It's impossible to rest the body while the mind is in turmoil. Despite knowing this, we continue to think incessantly—out of Habit—about the very things we should forget in order to rest.

We have the ability to control our thoughts. If Habit has been tethering us to exhausting thoughts, we must banish those thoughts from our minds. The only way to do this is by replacing them with thoughts of an opposite nature until Habit, which readily adapts to change, picks up and continues the kind of thought that we find most restful and delightful.

Repeating words that suggest rest will quickly calm a troubled mind and put it in a restful state. Mentally repeating the word "rest" is a valuable suggestion to restore balance in the nerve-centers and to focus attention (which is the function of suggestion) on what we desire to experience.

As long as thoughts and feelings suggest trouble and unhappiness, there can be no rest until sleep intervenes to temporarily quiet this irrational consciousness and restore the balance of power. The body is recharged with enough energy to allow us to continue worrying and depleting the new supply as before.

This is a poor use of the remarkable life-energy we possess. How eagerly would the forces at our disposal rise to the task of infusing the blood with courageous joy and filling each breath with the sweet essence of the joy of living if only they were given the right suggestions.

We should cultivate a habit of resting while working, instead of depleting our energy through exhausting thoughts. There can be no such thing as nervous prostration where restful suggestions are habitual. Auto-suggestion, where the conscious will is in control, is the most valuable form of suggestion. Suggestions given to hypnotized subjects place their nerve-centers under the control of another person's will, weakening the conscious will.

The old practice of displaying motivating mottos is based on the power of suggestion. If health and happiness were advertised as widely as disease, misery, and evil, it would reverse the negative impact of these harmful suggestions. If people focused as much on believing in and amplifying goodness as they do on suspecting and amplifying evil, goodness would prevail. Discussing the best qualities of others and offering more praise than blame would be wiser.

Any desirable trait of character can be cultivated, while any unworthy trait, whether inherited or acquired, can be eradicated. Traits of character are simply habits, and habits have remarkable potential, either as a threat or as a force for good. Habit always acts upon suggestions from thought and feeling, turning mental images into realities.

In a story by Gaboriau, his favorite detective, Lecoq, once astonished his employer, an astronomer, by revealing certain plans for committing crimes and escaping detection. Recognizing his talent, the astronomer advised him to pursue a career in law enforcement to use his skills for good rather than evil.

Words are not necessarily suggestions unless they focus attention on the ideas they represent. Simply looking at an inspiring motto repeatedly won't have an impact if its meaning doesn't resonate with us.

An attitude of despondency will evoke despondent thoughts and feelings, prompting the nerve-centers to create unhappy conditions. Holding the hands firmly while desiring something sends a strong suggestion to the nerve-centers to bring about the desired outcome. It's an attitude suggesting possession, which is what the nerve-centers need to act in a way that leads to possession. Suggestions of disease should not be entertained, as even the names of diseases can be suggestive if they strongly influence the mind.

It's a hopeful sign that the power of negative suggestions is being better understood, and that suggestions of health, happiness, and prosperity are replacing them to a greater extent than ever before.

If such positive suggestions can take root in the minds of those born into poverty, disease, and crime, they have the potential to lift these individuals out of their bondage to Habit and bring an end to this tragic cycle.

The White Plague, a Bugaboo

If you ask churchmen what they need most to save souls, they often reply, "Money; we can't get money." Similarly, doctors may say the same thing when asked what they need to cure diseases. "Give us millions," they say, "and we will eradicate tuberculosis from New York City."

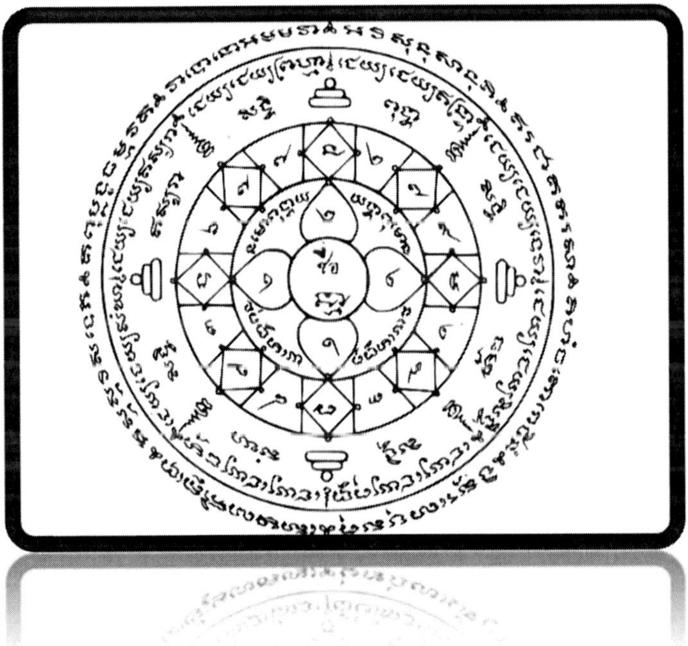

However, the truth is closer to what the church people sing: "Salvation's free for you and me." Salvation of both soul and body is indeed free. Each of us has a gold mine within us, but it needs to be worked to yield results. This inner gold mine is the "Kingdom of God" that Christ said is "within us." It's the power to create through the human nervous system the mental and physical conditions we desire.

Viewed through the lens of the law of Habit, tuberculosis appears as a mere bugaboo, much like the terrifying giant who made Jack o' the Beanstalk tremble with his ominous words. In rare cases where tuberculosis affects all body tissues, including the lungs, it's likely due to habits of thought responsible for most, if not all, insidious diseases. No amount of medical intervention like cod liver oil or fresh air can change this condition if the mind remains unhealthy. Constant distress or agitation of the mind, keeping the nerves tense, inevitably leads to disastrous results, with symptoms of disease being the most probable consequences.

However, the same power that causes mischief can also effect a cure. We simply need to cultivate the habit of focusing on restful and healthy conditions. We are the masters of the power represented by Habit and can direct it to build up healthy tissue.

This perspective was articulated by Miss Christine Brown of Roxbury, Mass., who has originated a new health cult based on "the sweet melodies and seductive strains of music." This is an excellent idea. Anything that can divert attention away from disease and suffering directs the nerve centers towards producing healthier conditions. Brown selects music that evokes nature, the outdoors, the sky, and the world of growing things, avoiding religious selections or anything that might induce melancholy or antagonistic feelings. While this is a step in the right direction, it's only the beginning. Patients must understand the importance of focusing their attention on happy and wholesome conditions, realizing that doing so is the only way to overcome disease.

"If people tell you that the sick can be cured without faith, don't believe them," says the leader of the Emmanuel movement. "Don't surround the sick with the atmosphere of death. No doubt, a good many die because their friends, by their manner, show that they expect them to die, and the sick ones do not want to cause any disappointment."

I think that in this statement is summed up most of the philosophy of cure, and that it is the recognition of these facts, rather than to the fresh air which their patients received, that Dr. Worcester and his followers have been able to cure twenty-five per cent of the cases of tuberculosis which they have treated in the last five years. To say that the sick should not be surrounded with an atmosphere of death implies the opposite. They should be surrounded with an atmosphere of health and buoyant life. It should be impressed upon their minds that they must cure themselves; that the same power, Habit, which, without knowing it, they are allowing to rule them, and drag them down, can be made to lift them up, and all that anyone can do for them is to help them to help themselves. They do not need to go away among strangers for a change of climate to do this. All they have to do is to change their habits, beginning with habits of thought, forget disease, fix their attention upon the most wholesome and happy conditions; and, of course, fresh air, proper food, and ordinary sanitary conditions are expected to assist wholesome mental conditions.

But it is not the fresh air that cures, nor is it a change of climate; it is getting away from old afferent stimuli to which the spinal nerve-centers will respond until stronger stimuli reach them from the brain centers.

The most common form of consumption, affecting the lungs, is a significant threat due to its widespread nature and constant increase. It typically begins with a "slight but persistent cough." Initially, the individual affected, known as the "consumptive," is not alarmed and feels that nothing is wrong with them—and indeed, there isn't. They are merely developing a habit of coughing, similar to how a drinker, in the early stages, may not be alarmed by their habit, not fully understanding the immense power of Habit.

The consumptive does not attribute their coughing to Habit. They perceive it as necessary to relieve the unpleasant sensation in their lungs. This sensation stimulates the spinal nerve-centers, prompting them to respond regularly by causing the muscle action resulting in a cough. The individual forming this habit of damaging their lung tissue in this manner does not realize it is simply a habit. They can control their spinal system and prevent it from responding to this stimulus, similar to any other habit, until the troublesome sensation diminishes, if not continuously stimulated by Habit.

As the habit grows, friends become anxious and often invoke the fear of tuberculosis to motivate action. However, the question of what to do remains. "Incurable" is a damaging suggestion associated with this condition. Perhaps, at great expense, the individual is sent away to some distant place, alone and miserable, wearing the cloak of tuberculosis without suspecting that their cough is a habit they can break. It's no surprise that they succumb—just as expected. They have become proficient coughers, damaging their lung tissue through this harmful and utterly useless practice, unaware that they possess the power to stop it by forming habits that promote lung tissue health.

I know of one case where a man, believed to be a victim of tuberculosis, had to refrain from coughing during the night to avoid disturbing a sick woman in the next room. Initially, he felt the urge to cough, as he had been accustomed to doing most of the night. Habit, like a tyrant, attempted in every way to compel his muscles to carry out the usual movements in response to the signals from his lungs. Holding the air in his lungs longer than usual provided relief, and by morning, he had not coughed. This led him to realize that it was possible to stop coughing. Once he embraced this idea, he broke the habit of coughing and recovered.

Habit often takes on the guise of an "evil spirit," compelling us to continue exhibiting symptoms of diseases. There's a story about a bicyclist who, while learning to ride, consistently collided with a particular telegraph pole. Despite having ample space on either side, he always ran into it because his attention was fixated on it out of fear. Muscular action tends to align with whatever the attention is focused on.

Even on one occasion when the bicyclist had passed the pole before mounting his bike, his thoughts were still consumed by it, causing him to circle back and collide with it. However, as the bicyclist becomes adept at riding, his spinal nerve-centers assume full control over his muscles, guiding them to avoid obstacles and maintain balance effortlessly. Habit allows him to perform these actions automatically, a stark contrast to when his brain-centers clumsily directed his movements. This same law of Habit, which previously caused him to collide with objects due to fear, becomes his ally once his nerve-centers are trained to respond consistently to other stimuli.

And so it is with the "consumptive." The same power that is destroying him can be harnessed to cure him—and there is no other cure. Despite all efforts made to save him, his fate ultimately lies in his own hands, and the first step towards recovery is adopting the right mental attitude. He must not merely hope, but know, that he can save himself. He must make Habit work for him, not against him, just as the bicyclist does. His practice will be of a different nature, but he must practice maintaining the right mental conditions, break the habit of coughing, and not allow his friends to frighten him with their somber expressions and detrimental suggestions.

I once heard a very sensible young woman, to whom someone had foolishly suggested she might have consumption, boldly declare, "I'll never have lung disease, for if I wanted to cough, I wouldn't." There is enough conviction in this emphatic statement, and the determination behind it, to effectively combat any disease.

The Mystery of Sleep

Sleep has always been one of life's great mysteries. The need for sleep is rightly classified among the basic human appetites. We crave sleep just as we crave food, for the sustenance of life.

D'Artagnan, the famous hero from Dumas' tales, used to remind his servant that "He who sleeps, dines," when money was scarce and the pantry empty. and so, his loyal servant Planchette, considering his master a paragon of wisdom and valor, followed suit and went to sleep accordingly. Hours of ordinary rest do not refresh the body as much as a few minutes of that mysterious unconscious state we call dreamless sleep.

In cases where an injury has exposed the brain, it has been observed that during dreamless sleep, it remains motionless. Dreams, on the other hand, agitate the brain in proportion to their vividness, and when awake, the motion is even greater. When stimulated by pain or anger, the brain protrudes significantly and "throbs tumultuously, in accordance with arterial pulsations." This suggests that during periods of activity, which always accompany consciousness, a greater supply of blood is directed to the brain, causing the protrusion mentioned.

In dreamless sleep, less blood flows to the brain, and the brain itself remains motionless as far as observable. Consciousness disappears with this cessation of brain activity. Where does it go? We can answer, in a Yankee fashion, with another question: Where does any form of energy go when it vanishes? Consciousness, being the result of rates of motion attributable to vibrations of brain matter and being "a specific stimulus to nerve matter just as light and sound are," must be a form of energy. Therefore, the same explanation for the disappearance of light and sound, namely "interference," must apply to consciousness.

Consciousness disappears with the cessation of brain activity and reappears with its renewal.

The question arises: why is this brain activity temporarily suspended with a regularity that suggests it is governed by law, and how is it brought about? There are only a few fundamental laws according to which the processes supporting life and development are carried out, all of which are controlled through the nervous system.

The principle of "afferent stimuli," centric action, and "efferent response" constitutes the first law, while the law of Habit, which dictates the tendency of the nerve-centers to respond to afferent stimuli, is the second and most significant. Additionally, there is a third law through which the higher nerve-centers inhibit or regulate the lower ones.

During consciousness, the brain centers restrain the lower spinal centers and keep them occupied with executing commands. Previously, the spinal system, as the original nervous system, only responded to afferent stimuli from external sources. However, the introduction of stimuli from higher nerve-centers demands greater effort and redirects a significant proportion of blood flow to the brain during its activity.

The spinal system had been accustomed to controlling the body independently, without interference from higher nerve-centers. However, these higher centers now issue complex commands, which often take years for the spinal system to execute accurately to achieve the desired outcomes.

W. Hanna Thompson compares the spinal system to a horse without a rider before the addition of the brain-centers. The addition of the brain-centers acts as a rider, directing the horse through various unfamiliar actions that strain its strength and require a portion of its resources.

The author of "Brain and Personality" suggests that during sleep, the rider voluntarily dismounts at regular intervals to rest and allow the horse to rest as well. However, the higher nerve-centers do not have exclusive control over the body's nerves. If the rider does not dismount and provide necessary rest, the horse will rebel and throw him off. The life-forces are stronger than the brain-forces and demand the liberty to which Habit has accustomed them, particularly when a balance of power needs restoration. The overall energy of the organism relies on maintaining this balance.

While consciousness governs the voluntary muscles, it disrupts the regularity of breathing and circulation. Excitement, labor, and various emotions and responsibilities associated with consciousness disturb the habitual regularity of life-processes, leading to fatigue due to this imbalance of power.

Notice the deep and steady breathing of a healthy sleeper. The primitive spinal nervous system has regained control. The brain centers are calm, allowing more blood to flow to the organs essential for sustaining life. Perhaps, like a masterful rider who has been thrown off by the horse, the higher nerve-centers have been relinquished, and the organism is at peace, reminiscent of a time when it operated solely on the spinal system. The life-forces have important tasks to accomplish, and they require freedom from interference from the brain centers to do so. Therefore, the law of inhibition enables them to assume full control of the body when signals of fatigue reach the vital nerve-centers.

When we voluntarily fall asleep, our thoughts gradually cease. Each brain center is silenced, and we progressively lose awareness of external stimuli. We concentrate solely on one goal: restful oblivion. If our attention remains fixed on this objective, insomnia becomes impossible. In cases of persistent wakefulness, the problem often arises from allowing our attention to wander or dwelling on thoughts that distract from the goal of rest. This tendency can develop into a habit, resulting in insomnia. However, it can be overcome by forming the habit of directing our attention towards the desired outcome: sleep.

However, sleep doesn't always provide us with refreshment. After a day filled with cares and excitement, we lay down to sleep, but our minds remain occupied with the activities that agitate them, preventing consciousness from being completely obliterated. Dreamland, with all its absurdities, often feels strangely real, and throughout history, significance has been attached to dreams. The belief in the significance of dreams can make them influential, and if a dream leaves a strong impression that becomes a suggestion, it may even seem prophetic. For instance, a young man from Chandler, Indiana, allowed a dream to consume his mind to the extent that he acted out its contents, shooting the girl who ended their engagement, her preferred suitor, and ultimately himself, just as he had dreamed. It's heartening to see the attention given to the danger of allowing harmful suggestions to dictate the activity of the nervous system, as highlighted in the newspaper article recounting this tragedy. This subject deserves the utmost attention because a dream or a thought can only become a suggestion if we allow it to deeply influence us.

Before sleep, the mind should be engaged with peaceful and joyful thoughts, gradually drifting into oblivion—the release from the day's turmoil.

During embryonic development, the life-forces, operating through the spinal system, maintain full control of the organism. The brain centers are dormant until birth, and the early stages of development are marked by adherence to fixed life-habits reminiscent of earlier evolutionary stages. The evolution of a human organism from a germ cell, resembling those that develop into onions, mirrors the progression from simpler life forms through the addition of new faculties. However, the faculty of consciousness adds complexity to the life-forces' burden, and infants sleep extensively as the spinal centers adapt to responding to stimuli from within the body. Despite yielding to the brain centers for a time, the spinal system periodically reclaims full control.

Children require more sleep than adults because their life-forces are actively engaged in building the organism, and through the law of inhibition, they retain the ability to assume control when fatigue signals them. Factors like anxiety, excitement, or habituation to prolonged sleep may contribute to individual differences in sleep requirements. The notion that the more one sleeps, the more one desires it suggests the influence of habit.

Fatigue, while often associated with work, is more significantly caused by anxiety and excitement, which disrupt the balance and lead to fatigue. A peaceful state of mind helps maintain balance, but consciousness, by its nature, is a disruptive element that the spinal system cannot sustain for prolonged periods.

Mental disturbance diverts blood from vital organs to sustain brain activity, which is not only futile but also harmful. When the brain requires more blood, it should be for the body's benefit, not detriment. The spinal system can tolerate this interference and increased demand on its resources only for a limited time.

The life-forces have their own tasks, and when the spinal system is excessively burdened by brain activity, they can cast off this burden and operate freely in their accustomed manner, reminiscent of earlier stages of evolution.

Our Brother, The Beast

There are thinkers who argue that human personality is fundamentally distinct from that of animals, if indeed animals can be said to possess personality at all. They tend to believe that animals lack personality and are merely living machines over which humans have dominion. However, I find this reasoning unpersuasive.

Anyone who has spent time with domestic animals can attest to the fact that each animal possesses its own unique individuality.

Just as no two humans are exactly alike in every respect, no two animals are identical in every aspect due to possessing slightly different organisms, despite sharing a general blueprint.

Animals serve different functions in the universe compared to humans, and they often fulfill their roles quite effectively. However, evolution has bestowed upon humans greater responsibilities and a broader scope of action, along with a more advanced organism. Some experts argue that the convolutions in the human brain are deeper and more numerous than those in the brains of other animals, while others suggest that the difference between the brain of a chimpanzee and that of a human is negligible. Yet, despite these similarities, humans are categorically distinct from animals.

While the brains of chimpanzees and humans may bear a striking resemblance, it is undeniable that humans occupy a unique position in the animal kingdom. Although there is greater similarity between humans and chimpanzees than between humans and other animals, there remains a significant difference between them. This distinction, the "last straw" of evolution, grants humans a broader understanding and consequently, greater power.

It is the possession of a heightened level of consciousness that elevates humans above their animal counterparts, and it is in the utilization of this elevated consciousness that humans can either rise higher than ordinary beings or sink lower than the lowest of beasts. What beast could inflict the misery and suffering that humans are capable of causing? I need not cite examples like the infamous Nero. Countless instances exist where humans, through their degradation of consciousness, have become despicable entities—a stain on the reputation of nature, making even the noble tiger in its jungle seem virtuous by comparison.

Animals possess all the knowledge necessary to fulfill their natural roles and have a language sufficient for their needs. Their consciousness does not extend beyond their immediate environment, nor do they possess the capacity for extensive reasoning. However, there is ample evidence to suggest that some of the more intelligent animals are capable of reasoning to a limited extent.

Animal desires are primarily focused on self-preservation and the perpetuation of the species. Their nerve centers are habituated, through heredity, to respond in specific ways to external stimuli, and these instinctual behaviors dominate much of their lives. Animals do not hunger for knowledge, as their consciousness is largely limited to their immediate needs. Nevertheless, I have observed in the eyes of an intelligent dog a look of attentiveness—a desire to comprehend and understand the subject of conversation it was listening to. Failing to understand, the dog would lie down contentedly and forget about it, but for a moment, there was a yearning for broader comprehension.

The thirst for knowledge is a defining characteristic of human nature. Our expanded consciousness provides us with glimpses of the vastness of the unknown, which we can never fully comprehend. Our supposed superiority over animals is merely a small step forward in evolution. Evolution has yet to achieve an organism that possesses full and complete consciousness.

Without the accumulated knowledge passed down through generations, our minds today would be barren wastelands, offering little more than survival under harsh conditions—a state not much different from that of animals or our primitive ancestors. However, even the most ignorant person today possesses knowledge that surpasses the wisdom of the wisest individuals from ancient times.

There is a growing aversion to certain savage customs that habit has ingrained into human behavior, signaling a progression toward a higher and more enlightened existence. It is becoming increasingly repugnant to kill and consume animals, with many recognizing it as a barbaric practice akin to cannibalism. Yet, shedding such habits, deeply ingrained over millennia, is a gradual process. Despite our proclaimed superiority and claim to an immortal soul, humans remain carnivorous animals.

I have witnessed the pitiful sight of an ignorant and cruel individual exerting dominance over a kind and loyal dog—kicking and mistreating the animal to assert their perceived superiority. Such individuals are painfully aware of their inferiority as humans and seize every opportunity to assert dominance over animals to compensate for it.

The horse, perhaps man's closest companion among animals, suffers greatly from its servitude to humans. While some may be fortunate to have kind masters, many face the prospect of being treated as mere machines, devoid of feelings and existing solely for human convenience.

A study of animal nature reveals creatures responsive to love and kindness, often more appreciative than fellow humans. My dog, for instance, trembles with excitement and distress when spoken to harshly, keenly sensing every tone of censure. His sensitive soul responds lovingly to a smile and affection.

Some have pondered the energy expended by dogs wagging their tails, wishing for an Edison to harness this supposed waste. However, tail wagging is a sign of happiness—a power for good, whether in a dog or any other creature. Encouraging a dog to wag its tail is a worthwhile use of energy.

Despite concerns about germs from household cats, the love exchanged with these dear creatures outweighs any potential risks. Dogs and cats, when treated with care and affection like children, become more intelligent and understanding, capable of profound devotion.

Animals, particularly dogs, are creatures of habit, and sudden disruptions can cause suffering and even danger. The profound bond between a dog and its master sometimes leads the dog to seek its master's grave and perish upon it—a testament to the gravity of habit disruption. Man, often preoccupied with his own affairs, may neglect the suffering he inflicts upon animals under his dominion.

Sitting comfortably before a fire on a cold winter night, man may deny entry to his dog and cat, considering them mere beasts without souls or the ability to help themselves. Yet, this indifference to their suffering contradicts beliefs in judgment and accountability before a higher power.

Anyone who believes they can inflict cruelty on helpless animals without consequence is deluded. Every act of suffering inflicted upon animals has a detrimental effect on the perpetrator, akin to a boomerang effect or a ball rebounding against a wall. This principle is a law of nature, unyielding to the power of wealth or human laws.

Whether the suffering is inflicted upon a human or an animal, the impact remains the same under this law. Those who mistreat defenseless animals are degraded and miserable, regardless of their outward appearances or religious affiliations. Even if someone holds esteemed positions like a Sabbath-school superintendent and boasts of their immortal soul, they remain degraded if they abuse animals.

Regarding the question of souls, we recognize their presence through the physical manifestation of their powers. Our animal brethren exhibit every indication of soul-life, with acute feelings and a strong will, albeit with limitations due to their physical mechanisms. While their intelligence may be lesser and their will less powerful than ours, their minds also contain "a little spark of the Almighty." Our greater intelligence should serve to enlighten and uplift the consciousness of our animal companions.

The Power of Expression

What do we not owe to the power of expression? Its wonders are unparalleled. The soul seeks to convey its knowledge and feelings in myriad ways, yet there are moments when words, our usual mode of expression, fall short of capturing the soul's depth. As Tennyson lamented, "I would that my tongue could utter the thoughts that arise in me."

The power of speech—how can we measure it or quantify its impact on life? It is the foundation of achievements, joys, and possibilities that elevate humanity above the realm of lower animals. Without speech, human progress would be stunted. Our ability to articulate thoughts through speech is among our most precious assets. Even our thoughts are influenced by speech; indeed, it has been said, "We think because we speak." Yet, we often fail to recognize the extent to which speech shapes our thoughts.

The vocal organs, through habit, can attain remarkable skill in articulation, producing 1,500 distinct sounds in a single minute. Unfortunately, we do not always appreciate this remarkable gift. It is not just the words we speak, but the tone in which we deliver them, that conveys the most meaning. It is crucial to cultivate tones of speech that are agreeable and soothing. Habitual use of harsh and unpleasant tones can have a detrimental effect on both our own nerves and those of others.

A person who scolds incessantly may attribute their irritability to physical factors, unaware that their physical condition is influenced by the habit of scolding itself. The jarring effect of harsh tones on the nerves can exacerbate physical ailments. This habit, like any other, must be addressed by cultivating opposite habits, such as adopting well-modulated and pleasing tones of voice, which can have a calming effect on the nerves.

The nervous system is highly sensitive to anything that disrupts harmony, and our overall well-being is contingent upon its condition. Expressing discordant thoughts and feelings ingrains harmful habits that can manifest as physical ailments. Therefore, it is essential to be mindful of the tones we use in speech and cultivate habits that promote harmony and well-being.

On the contrary, expressing harmonious feelings fosters the feeling itself, and when it becomes habitual, it can alleviate ailments caused by discordant thoughts and expressions. This is not mere speculation. It is evident that persistent expression of distressing feelings will inevitably lead to physical ailments, just as opposite conditions yield opposite effects. The adage "Actions speak louder than words" holds significant truth, and sometimes silence can convey more than speech.

Giving vent to anger may seem easier than restraining it, but exercising restraint is a demonstration of strength, whereas unrestrained expression dissipates our energy and weakens our capabilities. Conversely, we often overlook expressing feelings of love and kindness, assuming they will be understood, as speech is not our sole mode of expression.

Gestures are integral to communication, often conveying more meaning than words alone. A speaker who remains motionless while addressing an audience would struggle to captivate them; gestures are a natural accompaniment to our feelings and thoughts, particularly evident in children and emotionally expressive individuals.

A simple gesture—a shrug, a glance, a raised eyebrow—can convey volumes, but the eye communicates silently in a way words cannot match. The expressive power of the human eye is truly remarkable. Even an ordinary face can become beautiful when illuminated by eyes filled with love and enthusiasm, yet the message conveyed by the eyes may not always be genuine. Just as lips can speak falsely, so too can the eyes. A smiling face may mask villainy, while an innocent countenance may be nothing more than a façade.

Progression and Retrogression

Progression is inevitably followed by regression. Throughout history, nations have risen to great power only to later decline into obscurity. Yet, despite this cyclical pattern, knowledge and the overall advancement of the world continue to progress. Just as a whirlwind's destructive force eventually dissipates, giving way to stillness, life is succeeded by death, joy by sorrow, and vice versa. There is no continuous forward movement without moments of regression to temper or regulate it. This is exemplified by the circular motion of each particle within a wave, illustrating the principle of cycles that governs the universe.

While some argue that there is no inherent purpose in the universe, it remains challenging to convince humanity of this notion. Despite recent arguments supporting this proposition, such as G.T. Wrench's observation in "The Grammar of Life" that humans, like other animals, are subject to the rules of the universe, it does not necessarily follow that humans and their species lack ultimate aim or purpose.

Wrench posits that human purpose cannot be comprehended in terms of eternity. While it may be true that humans cannot sustain a continuous conscious purpose throughout eternity, we are nevertheless conscious of purpose in our lives. Without purpose in the universe, the concept itself would hold no meaning to us. We recognize purpose as an essential attribute of the mind, evident in all natural activities. The existence of rules which humans must adhere to further suggests purpose.

Mind operates within the framework of uniform laws across its various activities. Without purpose, the universe would descend into chaos rather than exist as an eternal and constantly transitioning entity composed of an unending series of cycles. Moreover, the absence of purpose would render the universe nonexistent.

The idea that progress cannot continue indefinitely without corresponding regression should not worry us excessively. The laws governing our existence assure us that the outcome of natural processes is nothing to fear. Humanity is evolving; we endeavor to improve not only our current situation but also that of future generations. We are moving towards a state of consciousness characterized by greater happiness. The practice of enslaving fellow humans has largely been left behind, and there are indications that even the enslavement of animals may soon be a thing of the past. Machinery is easing much of the burden of labor for both humans and animals, and large-scale cattle ranches are giving way to smaller farms. Some even argue for extending the right to immortality to animals.

While it is predicted that the Earth may eventually become uninhabitable for humans, it is also anticipated that the human species will have become extinct before this happens. Nature ensures that her creatures always have a means of meeting their needs. When one resource diminishes, another emerges to take its place. Every ending signifies a new beginning, and there are no abrupt transitions without something else to transition to. The human mind, our most cherished possession, remains undeterred by dire prophecies of world annihilation. It transcends all transitions and cannot be destroyed by them. As the famous saying goes, "It is better to die nobly than to live ignominiously and meanly." This resolute mind responds to all suggestions of catastrophe by affirming, "I lay down my life only to take it up again under different circumstances."

The question of immortality has always held great interest for humanity, and the belief in a continued existence after death has been a characteristic trait of human culture. Throughout history, this belief has often been intertwined with superstition, leading to the creation of various visions of the afterlife influenced by the customs and beliefs of different cultures.

In modern times, there is a growing tolerance and mutual respect between science and religion, allowing them to engage with the profound questions of life and immortality on common ground. This era sees superstition giving way to reason, and the emphasis on love and compassion replacing the intolerance and bigotry that have marked religious histories.

When religious institutions encourage individuals to use their reasoning abilities without fear of diverging from prescribed beliefs, it signals progress in the right direction. Attempting to impose our own narrow ideas onto the universe is a futile endeavor. Instead, we must confront reality as it is, rather than as we might wish it to be.

It is encouraging to hear statements like the following from a church leader, Dr. Worcester: "I believe that the church has erred in focusing almost exclusively on the normal, the well, the happy, and the rich—those who are innocent and good—and has forgotten the mission of Jesus Christ to show compassion for the poor, the sick, and the abnormal. The old notion that the church exists solely for the benefit of its members is becoming outdated. We will never save the world with that mindset. The traditional concept of the ministerial life is evolving. Ministers used to believe that their duty was solely to maintain their health, read, and deliver sermons with authority and force. That too is becoming outdated. People don't want authority and force. We should view our congregations as fellow-workers, like a family united in a common ideal."

When the church channels its efforts into practical Christianity rather than theoretical concepts, and adopts a more open-minded approach, its power and usefulness will increase.

Some have criticized the Emmanuel movement, claiming it only addresses minor nervous disorders and leaves more serious "chronic cases" to doctors. It would be interesting to assess the success of doctors in treating these chronic cases.

As the church progresses in this hopeful direction, science is also extending its hand to religion, seeking solid reasons to support a belief in immortality.

A learned physicist and electrician, E. Fournier D'Albe, B.Sc., A.R.C.Sc., has recently published a book titled "New Light on Immortality," wherein he argues that the soul indeed exists independently from the physical body and departs from it upon death. According to him, this soul-body consists of psychomeres, analogous to the cells of the physical body, and operates within a "psychic region" within the atmosphere, subject to natural laws.

Even if this assertion were proven true, it does not necessarily demonstrate immortality—an eternal existence without any interruption of conscious personality. Rather, it would imply that we must undergo another cycle of existence after completing this one.

And thus we progress along what appears to be "Life's intricate labyrinthine path," completing the cycle of our lives, much like the wave particle moves in its small circle, once again illustrating the fundamental principles of cycles and wave motion—an ascent followed by a return to the origin, to which we are forever connected—the universal mind.

The Business of Living

"To simply focus on accumulating energy within yourself, especially when in a calm state, will strengthen your energy until you feel fully empowered. This approach can also alleviate feelings of weariness and various symptoms. If you're not feeling well, infuse your system with new energy, and in just a few minutes, you'll feel rejuvenated."

I am grateful to Christian D. Larson for sharing this inspiring truth, as it holds significant value. We are coming to understand that our nerve centers are hubs of energy, presenting us with the challenge of utilizing them wisely. The human body, with its intricate inner forces, serves as the starting capital for our journey through life—a journey in which we are all inevitably involved. It is up to us whether this journey proves profitable or not. We can squander our capital like a saloonkeeper who consumes all his liquors and closes shop, or we can augment our reserves by diligently tending to our affairs and refraining from reckless behavior. A successful entrepreneur studies their business, approaches it with enthusiasm, and seizes every opportunity to grow their capital. While excitement and risk-taking may yield some results, it is the composed, calculated approach that ensures long-term success and sustainability."

There is nothing speculative or unreasonable about the method of increasing our energy capital. We all recognize the difference in power between someone who loses their composure and one who remains calm in challenging situations. Calmness is the initial step toward establishing balance in the nerve centers, which is the true secret behind accumulating energy. "In calmness is strength" is akin to saying "In unity is strength," as calmness represents a state of consciousness where the nerve centers act in harmony. It's akin to a concerted effort, where everyone pulls together, and when the nerve centers function in this manner while focusing on energy accumulation, success becomes inevitable. If attention were diverted elsewhere, the internal centers of force would, in this composed and determined state of consciousness, work just as inevitably to achieve different outcomes.

It's prudent for us to calmly assess our situation in the business of life and, if there's a simple and rational method for increasing our capital, we should be eager to learn and apply it. We must remember that while the body constitutes the more tangible part of our capital, it is indispensable and should be valued accordingly. The effectiveness of the forces we wield and control depends on the body. Whether we can dispense with the physical body in a subsequent existence is a matter not pertinent to our current experience of life. In this life, the human body plays a crucial role, and neglecting or despising it would be unwise.

Through the specific movements initiated by the nerve centers, we are able to actualize our desires. This innate tendency of the nerve centers to prompt specific movements, aimed at achieving the objects or conditions on which our attention is fixed, is a fundamental principle associated with the business of living. Understanding this principle is paramount, as all our thoughts and actions are rooted in it. Thoughts lead to actions, and each action contributes to achieving a desired purpose. While we may not immediately execute all necessary movements to manifest desired conditions, taking the first step sets us on the path towards eventual success. As Dr. Draper aptly stated, "Events, however great or sudden, are consequences of preparations long ago made."

We are constantly laying the groundwork for the future, whether we are aware of it or not. It is by seizing the opportunities presented to us in the present moment that we shape the future according to our desires. Happiness is a universal aspiration, and it is our entitlement to pursue it. However, we must understand how to attain it and avoid mistaking it for selfish pleasure. Just as individuals falter in times of prosperity by opting for the path of least resistance, they also stumble in their pursuit of happiness by seeking immediate gratification without considering the consequences.

When we align our actions with natural laws, nature lends its strength to ours, rendering us truly formidable. Conversely, resisting or defying these laws leads to confusion and defeat. An attitude of rebellion and antagonism only invites trouble and obstructs our path to happiness.

Sincerity is an indispensable trait in both personal and business affairs. Insincerity erodes trust, whereas a person of integrity maintains a sterling reputation. Deceptive individuals may fancy themselves clever, but ultimately they deceive no one more than themselves. A hypocrite is to humanity what an artificial gem is to genuine jewels. While falsehood may offer temporary pleasure, genuine happiness is fundamentally different, akin to the distinction between the Grand Canyon and an ordinary ravine. Acting deceitfully leads to self-contempt, a state incompatible with true happiness.

Human laws ideally should align with natural laws, although this isn't always the case. The complexities of life test our strength and judgment, but truth and honor are invaluable assets that we cannot afford to compromise. Indecision and weakness yield no results, but a resolute and unwavering determination sustains the nerve centers in their pursuit of achievement until the desired objective is attained.

We cannot afford to be disheartened when things don't unfold as expected. Often, the changes we desire occur when we least anticipate them. Maintaining an anxious mindset only serves to delay progress. This wisdom has been expressed in the old adage, "The watched pot never boils." If we anxiously await results and lament their delay, we disrupt the equilibrium necessary for achievement. We must let go of undesirable conditions and immerse ourselves in the consciousness of the best outcomes. This consciousness is a potent form of energy, akin to light or sound, and its nature significantly impacts our lives. It is Nature's most magnificent gift to us, and we must cherish it accordingly.

We should not allow the felicity of consciousness—the buoyancy of spirit observed in children and young animals—to diminish as we age. There's no reason why we can't maintain this vibrant life-energy throughout our lives. It's imprudent to squander our energies recklessly, subjecting our bodies to unnecessary strain and resorting to costly surgeries to rectify the damage.

The process of accumulating energy is delightful, akin to traversing pleasant paths on the road to happiness. We can rest while working, avoiding exhaustion or weariness. This strengthens not only our physical powers but also our soul's capacities, enabling us to reach beyond current limitations toward greater achievements, happiness, and success. Coupled with strong desire, this accumulation of energy brings unexpected improvements into our lives. We must ensure a generous supply of it if we wish to possess the power to achieve, enjoy, and succeed.

The boundless Universal Energy serves as the bank where our capital is deposited, unfailingly responding to our demands when made in accordance with natural laws. This journey of living offers us limitless possibilities, splendid opportunities, and delightful experiences, contrary to the misconception that it merely entails growing up, growing old, and dying.

~The End~